THE PURPOSES THAT DRIVE OUR *Lives* ARE GOD GIVEN

LET NO ONE TELL YOU OTHERWISE

*God wants us to 'to be fruitful, multiply,
fill the world and take dominion'.*

EDWIN P. NHLIZIYO SR.

Order this book online at www.trafford.com
or email orders@trafford.com

Most Trafford titles are also available at major online book retailers.

Printed in the United States of America.

ISBN: 978-1-4907-3094-3 (sc)
ISBN: 978-1-4907-3093-6 (e)

Trafford rev. 04/08/2014

 www.trafford.com

North America & international
toll-free: 1 888 232 4444 (USA & Canada)
fax: 812 355 4082

GUIDING PRINCIPLE

I would rather live my life as if there is a God, and die to find out there isn't, than live my life as if there isn't, and die to find out there is.

—Albert Camus

PREFACE

About Rick Warren's Book

With over 32 million copies of Pastor Rick Warren's book already sold, there is no doubt that this has become a Christian masterpiece, a must-read book that is now being used by many for Bible and other studies. It is influencing a whole generation of Christians, and its message is about our relationship with God.

In the process of delivering its message, it addresses issues about creation. In asking the question "What on earth am I here for?" it is clear we are talking about why and for what purpose God created the human species and placed it on earth. The book, by making statements such as "We were created to be like Jesus" or "You were created for God's pleasure," confirms its creation base.

My book examines some of these statements in the context of the Pastor's first three purposes why God put us here and asks the question; did the Pastor get it all wrong? Pastor Warren does give us license to ask God if we want to know our true purpose(s) on earth, and when we ask God by searching His Word, the purposes He has given us are different from the ones advanced by Rick Warren. That leads to the question, are the purposes given in the book *The Purpose Driven Life* even biblical?

The book is about what we need to do to enter the Kingdom of God. We are told that our lives, our purposes, and the things that drive our lives are not really important. We are told we are here to serve a higher purpose.

My argument, on the other hand, is that the higher purpose the Pastor is talking about finds expression in the lives people actually live.

There is no time-out from our lives in order to serve God, but everything we do by the second is part of that journey.

That higher purpose the Pastor talks about is not a stand-alone and separate goal of our lives but is a mere reflection of the lives we actually lead. It is the quality of the lives we live in the context of what the Bible tells us we ought to conduct our lives that counts.

The Bible says *"Don't let anyone look down on you because you are young, but set an example for the believers in speech, in life, in love, in faith and in purity."*[1] I mean, what we do on a day-to-day basis answers the question about serving the higher purpose. The two are inextricably intertwined; they are inseparable. You do not have to pause your actual life in order to serve God's higher purpose. You do this by living your life in full, but in obedience to God.

The eternity question the Pastor sets out to answer is defined by what we do during our lifetime here on earth, and as such is also inextricably intertwined with our very lives, it cannot be considered away from our everyday lives—the lives we actually lead.

Pastor Warren's book talks about our purpose here on earth as believers but rarely refers to creation. When we consult the Bible (ask God), the reasons God put us here on earth and His purposes for us are clearly spelled out. When I asked God by consulting the Bible "what on earth I was here for," the answer He provided was *"(I) God blessed them and said to them, 'Be fruitful and increase in number; fill the earth and subdue it. Rule over the fish in the sea and the birds in the sky and over every living creature that moves on the ground.'"*[2]

Pastor Warren fails to ground his purposes in this critical verse about creation for the Christian believer. In doing so, he both obscured and distorted his valuable message in parts of his book.

His five purposes in terms of biblical creation raise many questions. Are they relevant and valid in terms of God's intent when He created Adam and Eve? The Christian experience as we live it, which can be simply stated as to "live one's life in obedience to our Creator, and that when we succeed in doing this, our path to heaven (eternity) is assured," is rendered rather complex and literally unattainable for the average Joe, if one was to believe Pastor Warren. We are told we need to know our

---

[1]   1 Timothy 4:12
[2]   Genesis 1:28

purpose for being here on earth for our lives to have meaning and that our very own lives are not about us.

The problem with Rick Warren's contribution is that, taken in its entirety, it leaves an indelible message that we have to call time-out from life as we know it in order to serve God. He says the very things that drive our lives are not important, and there are other obscure things that should drive our lives if we want everlasting life. Reality is that the two cannot be separated. Worshipping God in spirit and in truth finds expression in what we do. I tried to reconcile the two with our lives minute by minute and second by second. To worship God is to love and honor Him, and to love God is to keep His commands.

For months after I started reading and rereading Pastor Warren's book, I kept pondering the issue of what we actually do here on earth to sustain ourselves and raise our families and what the Pastor says we ought to do, without much success. However, I finally figured it out. The basis of Pastor Warren's disconnect in this regard was that he failed to take into account that people do not start life out as believers. People start life as ordinary folks filled with the spirit of the world. It is this spirit that influences their lives. This spirit obeys all our lustful desires. Every member of the human race has this same spirit when they first come into this world. It is the same spirit that teaches a child to lie, to make excuses for bad behavior or blame others.

My children always blamed each other for minor transgressions around the house. When my youngest was too young to speak, he was blamed for everything that went wrong around the house. Of course, the moment he was old enough to defend himself, that escape was lost. The thing is nobody ever taught these children to lie. It is something we are born with. In fact, it is the job of the parent to teach the child to own up and tell the truth, for telling the truth that convicts oneself is something that goes against the grain.

Second, our lives have a universal purpose, and we all obey and serve that universal purpose. It was given to us by God at creation. There are a few exceptions of course, but on the whole, we obey these rules of nature. It is only at various points in our lives that we begin to seek a connection with the Christian God. That happens when we make that decision to be born again, not when we first come out of our mothers' womb. In our world today, only about a third of the human species have sought the Jesus Christ connection. For Christians, that is what we call the eternity question. That relationship with God begins when we are born again. This is the issue Warren's book deals with, though he did not clearly articulate it.

When he asks the question "What on earth am I here for?" he answers it by omitting the events in our lives from the day we are born to the day we are born again. He does not address our purposes and the things that drive our lives up to the day we are born again. This is the source of his "disconnect" with reality—a disconnect that is apparent in many of the things he says from Day 1 to at least Day 28.

His purposes No. 2 and No. 3 (Day 15 to 28) deal with areas that have made his book a best seller because he imparts useful insightful information about the family of God, the church. In fact, one can say with some justification that all five purposes of a purpose driven life the Pastor identifies are concerned only with one aspect of our human lives here on earth, and that is our spiritual lives—our quest for eternity. However, life is much more than our spiritual side, and it is what we do from the moment we wake up to the moment we go to bed that determines if we are obedient to the Almighty.

The Pastor's failure to articulate this at the outset is the basis of what I have termed a foundational disconnect between his message and the lives we actually live. The purpose and goals we set for ourselves in this life are the ones that determine whether we are true Christians or not.

Once one grasps the elements of this "disconnect," it becomes easier to understand Warren's message and integrate it into our daily lives. Otherwise, the Jesus message the book is concerned with is very simple to state, though difficult to live by. It is simply about love and obedience—obedience to the Creator by accepting Jesus Christ as our Lord and Savior. Our Adam nature, which is influenced primarily by the spirit of the world, always stands in the way, hence our struggles to be true Christians.

Before Jesus came to earth, the requirements for obedience were so difficult and onerous for most people. One can understand why Satan was called the prince of this world. Sinning ruled this world and still does. It is, after all, our very nature. God, in His infinite wisdom, sought to give humankind a better chance at eternity than under the old rules by making that ultimate sacrifice. The Bible says, *"For God so loved the world that he gave his one and only Son, that whosoever believes in him shall not perish but have eternal life."*[3]

God, after trying to build a model (obedient) nation on the basis of His chosen people, the Israelis and failing dismally at the effort, finally figured out an easier way for His human creations to fellowship with Him and have everlasting life. He provided us with an alternative path to heaven which did not depend on our total obedience. His new approach to saving us just like the old does not permit sin, but unlike the old, it justifies (excuses) it. We say we are justified by the blood of Jesus because, when Jesus was crucified and then resurrected, He took our sins—past, present, and future—with Him. Our sins were forgiven.

All God has asked of us in return is that (1) we accept His one and only begotten son as our Lord and Savior; (2) that we read and meditate on His Word (the Bible) to discover His will for us and to know the difference between right and wrong; (3) that we obey His precepts; and (4) that when we do the wrong thing (sin), we confess and ask Him for forgiveness. We call this His Grace, a free gift from God. It is this simple formula that will get us to heaven. It is not the mumbo jumbo that Christian preachers scream about in churches throughout the world. It is not the myriad of requirements that we find in Pastor Warren's book that will do the trick. It is that simple, and some of us continue to wonder why the other two thirds of humanity (non-Christian) have not yet figured this simple truth out.

It is with the above in mind that I am inviting you to examine Pastor Rick Warren's *The Purpose Driven Life* all over again with a different perspective.

---

[3]   John 3:16

PROLOGUE

The Human Life Cycle

The Natural Order

Simply stated, the human life cycle has three primary steps. You are (1) born, (2) you live, and (3) you die. Life is what you experience from the day you are born to the day you die. That is what the Bible calls a lifetime[4] and that happens to be my reality.

Reading Pastor Rick Warren's book, our life experience here on earth and the afterlife are treated as a single lifetime, and our purposes here on earth are focused on the desire to go to heaven. That is a distorted way of looking at life for it denies reality. To live a Jesus-like life means living your life here on earth (reality) in obedience to God. It is about carrying out your day-to-day chores and activities, which include doing everything your heart desires as long as it does not displease God.

The key to obedience is to know behaviors that displease your Maker and to avoid them. You get that information from reading your Bible. If you can do this, you should have no fears or anxieties about going to heaven when you die.

This result will occur whether you know your true purpose(s) in life or not. Knowing your purpose is, therefore, not a determining factor whether or not you're going to heaven. Since our lives here on earth began with creation (Genesis 1:28), it would seem logical that anyone talking about a purpose driven life here on earth would begin that discourse with creation. I mean God's creation of the human species in His own image

---

4   Ecclesiastes 3:12 NASB

and what His stated purpose(s) were. According to the Christian Bible, God's purposes were that we:

(1) be fruitful;
(2) multiply;
(3) fill the earth;
(4) subdue it (the earth); and
(5) take dominion over all his other creations.

If we are genuinely looking for a purpose to our lives here on earth, shouldn't this be the best place to start?

I am sure we can derive the purposes and subpurposes of our lives from what God intended for us to accomplish on this earth. However, somewhere along this journey we call life, another purpose, a purpose not explicitly stated by God, emerges. It is the realization by some that they need to connect with their Creator. Let us call this the "Jesus connection" for Christian believers. When this happens, we seek Jesus by accepting Him as our Lord and Savior, and we are baptized. We are born again.

When we start with creation as I have done below, our fourth purpose for a purpose driven life is to seek Jesus Christ as our Lord and Savior. We can also call this our quest for eternity, and when one really thinks about it, that is what Pastor Rick Warren's book was all about. The foundation scripture for all this is Genesis 1:28.

God had a purpose for His creations, i.e., He wanted us to do something. A purpose driven life for humankind has to derive from what God intended for us. The result is what Greek philosophers, such as Socrates and Pluto, called the natural order of things. I believe that, by examining this natural order of life, we can easily arrive at what a purpose driven life is or should be about.

One can arrive at the purposes of life in a variety of ways on the basis of the foundation scripture. One can also divide and subdivide the resulting purposes into as many purposes as they want. Those purposes are, however, going to be very different from the ones suggested by Pastor Warren. This is so because they are an expression of the reality of the life you are leading right now.

THE HUMAN LIFE CYCLE CHART

The human life cycle begins with a birth and ends with a death. God, however, started the human life cycle with a male (Adam) who was past puberty and followed this by creating a woman (Eve) who was also past puberty. The purpose was to join man and woman and begin the procreation cycle. When Adam and Eve came together and became one flesh, there was a birth—the first biological birth of the human species.

That remains the natural order for the human species and the whole animal world for that matter. That is how we multiply. I accomplished God's purpose to multiply by marrying a person of the opposite sex and having babies.

Just as God had His purpose for creating us, He also gave us a purpose, which was to care and raise those babies until they were of age.

God's other purpose was for us to inhabit the earth. To do that, God spread His human creations to all parts of the world. This migration began after the flood with the descendants of Noah. We see that to multiply, one needs to get (1) a partner of the opposite sex and (2) have children. However, to have a wife means to have a home; to have children means to have resources to feed and nurture them until at least age eighteen in today's America.

Does anyone with children really have a problem answering the question "What on earth am I here for?"

God has provided us with resources with which to support our families, but we have to subdue them, which means to harness them for our benefit. It means to take dominion of all living things, all of God's riches on earth, for our own survival as a species.

We are born, we grow, we become adults, we start families, we become grandparents, and we die. That is a lifetime. It does not include life in the hereafter. That is the natural order that we all go through whether we are Christian, Jewish, Muslim, Buddhist, or Agnostics. What separates us as Christians is that, at some point, we made the decision to seek a God connection. That phase of our lives begins when we are born again. Pastor Warren's book is really about this area of our lives.

If we were to create a human life cycle chart, it might look something like the one below.

TYPICAL LIFE CYCLE

Age	Stage	Goal
0-3	In-Home Learning	Recognition
4-18	In-School Learning	Primary thru high school
19-22	In College Learning/Work	Acquire job skills
23-26	Post Graduate/Work	Begin career/Look for life partner
27-65	Work + Start Family	Develop career/Raise a family
66-90	Retirement	Giving back to society

We can easily summarize a typical life cycle for today's man (and woman), and what we might find is that, from roughly age four to about twenty-two, the major purpose of our lives is education. If you are living a purpose driven life, we would expect to find you in school when you are in this age group. If you are between age eighteen and twenty-four, we would expect you to be in college or in the workforce.

If we asked a typical eighteen-year-old what his or her purpose in life was, the answer would most likely be about getting good grades and going to college. For a parent, a major purpose at that time in their child's development would be to educate the child. That also means to have the resources for junior to go to college.

If we encountered the same eighteen-year-old five years later, the new young adult might be talking about getting a well-paying job. Some might be talking about getting married and having children as a not so distant future goal. Yet if you asked them, a mere three years beyond their twenty-third birthday, the "getting married and starting a family" part would become even more pronounced especially for women.

Likewise, if we asked a typical forty-year-old the same question, the answer might be their goal in life is to excel in their profession, raise children, and make sure they have a good education. If we asked the same man or woman the same question at sixty, he/she might mention retirement and enjoying their grandchildren and the rest of their natural lives.

Even people who still have mountains to climb at that age, they will probably not harp on them that much signaling the usually unspoken reality by most that within the next twenty-five years after sixty the majority will most likely be gone from this earth. That is life; that is reality; that is the natural order of things.

This analysis suggests that some purposes of our lives remain the same, while others change with time. The things that drive our lives here on earth are not static but also change with time, depending on the individual's age and circumstances. Thus, when I was in college, the things that drove my life were tied to the need to graduate with good grades and to get a well-paying job. When I got my first job after college, the primary driver changed. I was now trying to develop a career and to excel at it.

The moment one starts working, however, the issue of marriage also begins to wag its tail, if it was not already there. The reason for this is because we are now in the process of separating from Mom and Dad and creating a family unit of our own. We are never really conscious of where we are headed, but it all starts with dating—a boy and a girl pairing off, becoming inseparable, getting married or living together are just a matter of time. Once this step is accomplished, children of course soon follow.

The real story is that, while we travel life's journey, we face many challenges. However, for each person, whether they are Jewish, Christian, Muslim, or other religion, there is one constant with few exceptions—everyone wants to get married and have children. Why is that?

Second, no one can deny that the life span for the average person on earth today is roughly between seventy and ninety years. There are variations of course depending on the country one lives in and the longevity of the individual concerned. In the United States of America, the average life expectancy is eighty-three, and it remains true that very few people make it past ninety.

Our discussions about human life should be concerned with how we spend the years God allows us to be here on earth, the years between birth and death, that is our lifetime. Whether we go to heaven depends on what we do here on earth. The purposes that will enable us to get to heaven are thus inextricably intertwined with our human (God given) purposes here on earth and the things that drive us.

RICK WARREN'S FIVE PURPOSES

Many people have read Pastor Rick Warren's book, and the questions many readers are asking today have a lot to do with the five purposes the Pastor advanced as the reasons why God placed us here on earth. They are:
(1) You were planned for God's pleasure.
(2) You were formed for God's family.
(3) You were created to become like Jesus.
(4) You were shaped for serving God.
(5) You were made for a mission.

On page 21 of the Pastor's book (revised edition), he makes the statement that "if you want to know why you were placed on this planet, you must begin with God." Therefore when we answer the question "What on earth am I here for?" it was my expectation that the answer would come directly from the Bible, which is how we ask God for answers nowadays. The Bible, as usual, rarely fails to provide an answer.

There is of course another possibility, and those of us who watch the Bible channels on TV often hear many pastors claiming God told them this and that. Since these claims, coming as they do from eminent religious people are probably true we need not detain ourselves discussing them other than to point out that they remain largely unverifiable. We, therefore, should leave that subject alone for purposes of this book and its message.

It is, however, sufficient to say that even in the Old Testament times, only a few special people were ever able to speak to God like that. Since the last canon in the Bible was finalized (Revelations in AD 95-96), it is true that God has only spoken to people through the Bible.

Just remember, however, that there is always a thin line between reality, and the delusions of our own minds in this area of our spiritual lives. If God still speaks to people in the manner He did with Job, Moses, Abraham, and the rest of His special friends, He has given us tools with which to test the veracity of their claims. The Bible is rather explicit on this point. It says, *"The prophets are prophesying lies in my name. I have not sent them or appointed them or spoken to them. They are prophesying to you false visions, divinations, idolatries, and the delusions of their own minds."*[5] That's a pretty strong statement coming as it does from God Himself.

---

5   Jeremiah 14:14

Christian preachers should take a page from Dr. Martin Luther King and say it like it is, "I had a dream . . ." and not claim God told me this and that.

In the Gospel of John, we are also told, *"Do not believe every spirit, but test the spirits to see whether they are from God, because many false prophets have gone out into the world."*[6] For purposes of this book, however, we will only look to the Bible when we want God to tell us something.

My purpose in writing this book in addition to offering comments and ideas on Pastor Rick Warren's book is also to emphasize the need to seek God and His will for us only through prayer and the Bible. If we accept, therefore, that the reasons we human beings were created in His image and placed on this planet are biblical, it should not be difficult for us to discover our true purpose(s) on earth from the Bible, specifically the book of Genesis.

My book seeks to answer the Pastor's question "What on earth am I here for?" and answer it from this biblical angle. When we do that, we come up with God's purposes that are perfectly aligned with life as we experience it—life as we live it. They are practical and true to life.

Anyone reading this can easily determine if they have lived life in accordance with God's purposes. The purposes are inescapable and apply to everyone across the board irrespective of their religion or nationality or level of intelligence. These are the usual life cycle experiences to which we all are subject. Creation began with man and woman. The Bible says God "created us man and woman" with a mission to multiply and to be fruitful. It was at this point in the human life cycle that God chose as our beginning.

On page 76 of the Pastor's book, he makes reference to what God said to Noah about the creation verse. The Pastor says God told Noah, "It's time to get on with your life! Do the things I designed humans to do. Make love to your spouse. Have babies. Raise families. Plant crops and eat meals. Be humans. That is what I made you to be!" This shows that the Pastor was aware of God's purposes for putting us here. Therefore, the answer to his question "What on earth am I here for?" was staring him straight in the face. Then why didn't he develop his purposes directly from this scripture? The answer is the substance of the Pastor's disconnect, which I address throughout this book.

---

[6]   1 John 4:1

Our analysis of the human life cycle begins at the point when Adam finds his Eve and is ready to start procreating. If you never married (or found yourself a life partner), I am not judging you. My point is there is a natural order to life, *but* as in all things, there are exceptions.

What then were God's purposes when He created the human species? The order in which the following purposes are presented is based on the Adam and Eve situation, but that is not important.

WHY GOD CREATED US

Purpose #1: To Inhabit the Earth

God's purpose was for us to inhabit the earth. He did that when He created Adam and Eve. To fill the earth, He decided to do it through procreation. It remains the same today. We need to get someone of the opposite sex (Adam and Eve) and become one flesh and have children. Our reference scripture for this says, *"Therefore a man shall leave his father and mother and be joined to his wife, and they shall become one."*[7]

I am not arguing that those who never married have sinned, but I am simply saying, if God put us on this earth to multiply and populate the earth, then not marrying and starting a family is inconsistent with God's design.

It is also a fact that many people today choose to skip the marrying part and go directly to becoming one flesh with a person of their choice, having children and raising them. Sin is involved in these situations if you are a Christian, but the Christian God is always ready and willing to forgive if one repents. In this situation, repentance would mean marrying the one you are with.

There are societies in this world where marriage in the legal or religious sense is not a requirement. Generally speaking, there is some type of ceremony marking the coming together of the couple. However, even in these cases, if we accept the proposition that the vow of marriage is between a man and a woman, then the same considerations apply. God

---

[7]   Genesis 2:24

says whatever we bind on earth will be bound in heaven,[8] but let me warn you, the verse might not apply here. Check it out with your pastor.

Either way, it does not affect our human life cycle analysis but will come into play with respect to our Purpose #4 below, that is, if you're a Christian.

Purpose #2: To Bear and Raise a Family (Ages Puberty [13] to Menopause [45] for Eve)

In our scheme of things and in accordance with God's design, children are a natural consequence of man and a woman living together as husband and wife. There are exceptions of course, but they are outside God's design. On the whole, though we can admit that a goodly percentage of people of age do get married and start a family. A smaller percentage manages to have children out of wedlock. Based on our present understanding of the scriptures, these people have committed a sin if they claim to be Christians. They are, therefore, invited to repent their sin by marrying that life partner and then ask God for forgiveness.

Raising a family entails not only feeding them but nurturing the new born until he/she can stand on his/her own feet. The length of this dependence can last beyond the eighteen years we use as the age of majority in this country.

Purpose #3: To Lead a Fruitful and Productive Life (Harnessing God's Resources)

You are going to need a source of income. We prepare for our careers by first having a good education—first under the guidance of our parents followed by a succession of teachers who continue the process. This preparation, when done well, increases our chances of getting a better-paying job when we become of age. From roughly age four through age twenty-two, we are involved with one form of learning and training or another.

However, others prepare for the future better than others. In America, the children who make it into medical school on average fare

---

[8]   Matthew 18:

the best the rest of their lives compared to the children who drop out of high school. This latter group is clearly at the other end of the spectrum.

These children, even though they do not realize it, they are most likely sentencing themselves to mediocre lives the rest of their lives. The curse of life thus begins early in the lives of these children. On an average, a child who dislikes school is well on his/her way to a mediocre life. It is more so for boys than for girls because, in our day and age, girls have a better chance of marrying up the economic social ladder than boys.

The problem with society today is we are generally unable to convey this truth to our children at an early-enough age to make a difference. Yet role models for a mediocre life are all around us.

There is another element to this purpose that could be shown as a separate purpose for us, if one chooses to do so. God wants us to take dominion over all His other creations and harness them as a resource to sustain us. It is this purpose that provides us jobs and the income we need to support our families. According to the Bible, those who cannot provide for their families have denied the faith and are worse than unbelievers.[9] Others might choose to deal with this as a separate purpose because taking dominion means we manage the earth's resources which have been entrusted to us by God.

Purpose #4: To Seek the God Connection

Seeking the God connection involves obedience to our Creator. It is an overarching purpose that applies to all members of the human race. It is not explicitly stated in Genesis 1:28, but we know of it from the verse that says, *"And to Adam he said, 'Because you have listened to the voice of your wife and have eaten of the tree of which I commanded you, You shall not eat of it [you disobeyed], cursed is the ground because of you; in pain you shall eat of it all the days of your life; thorns and thistles it shall bring forth for you; and you shall eat the plants of the field."*[10]

We learn from this passage that everything we do is subject to this purpose, especially if one is a Christian, a Jew, or a Muslim. Everything we do should be done in total obedience to God. This is the God factor

---

[9]   1 Timothy 5:8

[10]   Genesis 3:17

that we should be talking about and passing on to our children. It is a constant from the day we are born to the day we die.

The Bible says it best when we read, *"As obedient children, do not conform to the evil desires you had when you lived in ignorance."*[11] Pastor Rick Warren's book is really about this issue, and he has focused on the followers of Jesus Christ only. However, this part of our lives does not really begin at birth but begins at some point in the individual's life—the point at which they decide to accept Jesus as their Lord and Savior. For most people, their purposes in this life and the things that drive their lives are already set.

When one is born again, one might make some adjustments to the things that drive their lives or their purposes, but there is no wholesale overhaul of their lives. Instead of playing golf on Sunday, they might as well choose to go to church. Instead of extramarital relationships, they might opt for fidelity in marriage as they cultivate their heart fields by removing the rocky places, the hard places (roadside), and the thorny places. That is the exact message Jesus sought to convey in the Parable of the Sower.[12]

Pastor Warren has done a wonderful job of dealing with this God connection, i.e., our quest for eternity, but it does not supplant the important things that drive our lives. It simply adds a new dimension to it that forces us to make adjustments to our lives so they become Jesus-like. He failed to recognize that our daily lives here on earth are inextricably intertwined with our quest for eternity and are the primary determinant whether we go to heaven or to hell.

Purpose #5: To Give Back

Apostle Paul says, *"In everything I did, I showed you that by this kind of hard work we must help the weak, remembering the words the Lord Jesus himself said: 'It is more blessed to give than to receive.'"*[13]

The Bible encourages us to give. We give in a variety of ways throughout our sojourn here on earth. Those who have succeeded materially demonstrate this attribute the most. This is the time in life

---

[11] 1 Peter 1:14

[12] Luke 8:1-15

[13] Acts 20:35

when our goals have been met. We have passed the torch to the next generation in the sense that our children are now themselves parents. You have done your bit for society. You're now approaching your twilight years. This is the time to give back if God has so blessed you, and you have the time and the means to do so.

When I think of the best examples of giving back in our lifetime, I think of two American presidents—Jimmy Carter and Bill Clinton. Both came from humble beginnings, but Bill Clinton has excelled. He equipped himself for his mission on earth through excellence in education, en route to becoming the president of the United States.

Having excelled in that role, as president of the United States, we all saw him amass a small fortune for himself and his family. Now as the elder statesman, he is seen all around the globe helping the underprivileged through the various charities he is associated with.

Now there are going to be some people who will focus on his past weaknesses, but the truth is, the Christian God is so forgiving. If this man has made his peace with his God, then all his sins—past, present, and future—are forgiven. He will probably be in the welcoming committee if there is indeed a heaven up there.

Like the biblical David who was prone to error throughout his public life, no one ever doubted where Bill Clinton's heart was. He was for the poor and disadvantaged, the same as Jesus Christ. If he has repented, forgiven his enemies and accepted Jesus Christ as his Lord and Savior, this man is bound for heaven. (I almost said, so said the Lord, but I quickly remembered that I am no prophet.)

There are many others in his age group like Bono (Paul David Hewson) who have chosen to associate themselves with the plight of the disadvantaged. They have not devoted their time and wealth to the fun and games generally associated with some of Hollywood's rich folk. These people volunteer to help the poor in appropriate ways, depending on their own personal situations.

Unfortunately, there are many more like-minded people who have not been so blessed and go to the grave still fighting just to make ends meet, because while God may have blessed them in many other ways, He did not bless them with material things. Others give back by volunteering their time, but they never had the opportunity to become financially independent in this life.

INTRODUCTION

Rick Warren's book, *The Purpose Driven Life*, has resonated with a great number of Christians and non-Christians alike worldwide. The book clearly brings out many biblical truths that resonate with many readers. The book deals with matters we are all too familiar with, especially if one is a Christian.

For those of us who dab as lay preachers in our churches, we now use the book not only to teach others but also to find suitable material for our sermons. That says a lot for the book and its author.

The book touched me in a variety of ways.

First and foremost is the fact that I have done a lot of research centered round the book's message, and in many areas, I found verses that reversed the way I had previously read and interpreted the scriptures. I had taken certain verses in the Bible as gospel, only to discover after researching some of them that I was mistaken. I also thought I understood certain overused passages from the Bible without really comprehending.

A good example of this is the passage in the Bible that says, *"For he chose us in him before the creation of the world to be holy and blameless in his sight. In love he predestined us for adoption to sonship through Jesus Christ, in accordance with his pleasure and will—to the praise of his glorious grace which he has freely given us in the one he loves."*[14] This is the type of scripture one reads without comprehending until something forces you to study it further. It talks about being predestined, and when you research that one word *predestination*, it is like opening a biblical Pandora's box of sorts.

---

[14] Ephesians 1:4-6

The Apostle Paul says in the same passage that God "chose us in him before creation of the world," something that causes you to realize that God's concept of time is different from ours. How could He have chosen the Apostles and His followers (disciples) before He created the world?

I also read about the "great commission" without fully understanding what was involved here. This is where Jesus passes His power to His disciples. When the great commission is read from the Gospel of Mark, it is easy to see how significant this was. The operative verse says, *"He said to them, 'Go into all the world and preach the gospel to all creation. Whoever believes and is baptized will be saved, but whoever does not believe will be condemned. And these signs will accompany those who believe: In my name they will drive out demons; they will speak in new tongues; they will pick up snakes with their hands; and when they drink deadly poison, it will not hurt them at all; they will place their hands on sick people, and they will get well.'"*[15] This is the license all of us believers have to evangelize and take the Good News to all the nations. It is also our authority to heal the sick and cast out demons in His name.

In the process of reading his book and studying the Bible, I also discovered the truth about many Bible concepts I had previously thought I understood, only to learn yet again that I was wrong.

I found myself spending days researching topics such as "speaking in tongues" being "filled by the Holy Spirit," "once saved always saved," "predestination," "God's will," "God's plan for me," "many are called but few are chosen," and many more. These issues only served to provoke me into further study of the Bible and related literature. All this was clearly provoked by reading the Pastor's book.

I struggled with the Pastor's view that God's family is more important than my natural family—something I have devoted considerable space in a later chapter. The book also got me into the habit of making notes to record my first reactions and impressions of the material I was reading for the first time. It was from these notes that the idea for this book first came to me.

I am not writing this book because I necessarily disagree with what Pastor Rick Warren had to say. The reality is because the book gave me new insights into what it means to be a Christian, I realized that I could not reconcile some of the things the book had to say with my own

[15]   Mark 16:15-18

personal perspective on the Bible. I saw conflict between life as I live it and my quest for everlasting life. In this sense, the book has been a useful resource for me, but I also felt that the rich ideas it offers in some areas defied practical application to my life.

A major failing in my view was that the book ignored the reality that its audience lives real and ordinary lives and that it is within that context that they look to the Almighty for help and guidance to navigate their way through this life. Yet the book's basic message seemed to be that real life pressures to provide for our families are not the big issues driving our lives.

How so Mr. Pastor, I kept asking as I read on?

TRUE CHRISTIAN PRACTICE

The Pastor's book makes the argument that the desire to go to heaven is or should be our foremost consideration. I did not see that as reality at all. At best, the desire to go to heaven is an integral part of the lives we live here on earth. Going to heaven is simply the reward we get for living our lives in obedience to God.

Likewise, our lives are driven by the very things that the Pastor claims are not the most important. I liken this life's journey with a race. You can sit in class and learn about the theory of running a race, but if you do not participate in the actual race, you cannot expect to get to the finish line. Likewise, if you do not live your life according to God's rules, you should not expect to go to heaven. It is that simple.

Eternity is just the reward for living an obedient life here on earth, and the two are inextricably intertwined. The real message of the book should have been that if we can meet our real-life responsibilities (obligations) in complete obedience to God, chances are we will end up in heaven. True Christianity is that simple.

It gets even simpler when we realize that, even though God wants us to avoid sin, when we do sin, He does not condemn us but offers us forgiveness if we acknowledge our transgression and ask Him to forgive us. The Christian God offers us this free gift (His grace) once we accept His son Jesus Christ as our Lord and Savior. John 3:16 is of course our starting point as Christians.

There are conditions, however, to forgiveness. God's grace might not operate in our favor if (1) we blaspheme the Holy Spirit; (2) we fail to forgive those who trespass against us; and (3) we fail to acknowledge our mistakes and to ask God for forgiveness so we will not die with unconfessed sins.

There are two other conditions that need to be satisfied as well for us to be forgiven. The first says, *"You cannot sin continually if you want to remain under God's grace."*[16] Note that the Bible does not say you will not sin because you have accepted Jesus as your Lord and Savior, but only that sin shall no longer have dominion over you. The difference between the two is that a believer knows when he/she has sinned and is quick to go before the Throne of God and ask for forgiveness, while the unbeliever lives by the flesh. They do whatever pleases them. There is literally no right or wrong in their lives, and everything is for their pleasure.

The second condition says you should forgive your brother or sister who sins against you "seventy times seven . . ." (NIT).[17] The unanswered question is "Was Jesus telling us there is a limit to forgiveness or telling us the very opposite, i.e., that there is no limit to forgiveness?" If His message was that there is a limit to forgiveness, was the limit 490 (7 x 70)?

It would seem, therefore, that the challenge in Christianity (the Jesus thing) is not so much in the message itself, for the message is actually very simple and straightforward. The challenge is in our inability to obey God, or to put it in another way, to actually do His Word.

God realized more than 2,000 years ago that His human creations were incapable of living sinless lives. He responded by giving us a new covenant—a covenant that offered us an alternative way into His Kingdom. All we had to do is live under the cross, and we will be saved.

---

[16] Romans 6:1-2
[17] Matthew 18:22

RICK WARREN'S

What On Earth Am I Here For?

(DAY 1 TO DAY 7)

CHAPTER 1

It All Starts with God

In this chapter, we will learn that the purpose of life is not about us but is about our Creator. To discover our purpose, therefore, we need a revelation from God. He is the starting point.

When I first ordered a copy of Pastor Rick Warren's much read book, *The Purpose Driven Life*, my decision was based on what others who had read the book told me. I had also read a number of reviews, and I felt I was missing out on the Pastor's insightful message. I was not disappointed on this score. His book was a refreshing look on Christianity and church practices in general. Yet upon reflection, I started to question some statements in the book including the one that says, "It's not about you."

IS LIFE ON EARTH NOT ABOUT ME?

The Pastor argues that our very life experience here on earth is not about us. It's not about our personal fulfillment or happiness. He says it's far greater than our families. In short, we are here on earth to serve a greater purpose—God's purpose.

I could not agree more with the idea that we are here to serve God's purpose. As a Christian, I had always believed that God's purpose for us on this earth was as He stated it in Genesis 1:28: (1) To be fruitful; (2)

to multiply and (3) fill the earth; (4) to subdue the earth, and (5) to take dominion over all His other creations. It is also clear from the above that God's purposes were about us. Multiplying is clearly about me (and you). Then what was I missing from the Pastor's message?

What I was missing or still missing is what the Pastor's book is about. The Pastor leads us for some forty days on a mysterious search for something we all thought we had and knew until he told us we didn't know—he told us we did not know God's purpose for us on this earth.

If God's purpose is other than what God stated in the Bible, then what is it? According to scripture, God's purpose for us is as stated in Genesis 1:28. It is about procreation and filling the earth. We are told in Genesis 9:18-29 that all nations were peopled by the descendants of Noah. That explains how the earth was eventually filled.

It is also about taking dominion over all God's other creations on earth.

It is about obeying Him, honoring Him, and glorifying His name. In fact, we glorify Him when we live lives that exude the fruit of the spirit. That is all God ever wanted from us. It is about living lives anchored in obedience. It is about the family, your family, my family. It is also about striving to sustain yourself and to take care of your household and being fruitful in all areas of your life.

The Pastor, after making a series of questionable statements, says if we need to know our purpose on earth, we should not do that by speculating; but we should do it through revelation. The answer is to be found in the Bible. The Pastor says, "We can turn to what God has revealed about life in His Word." However, just before I could say "Bravo Pastor Warren!" the Pastor went off on a tangent again. He now claimed that his five purposes were clearly revealed in the Bible by God.

Last I looked, however, the Bible said nothing about the Pastor's five purposes for us being here on earth. As I have said before, God has explicitly stated His purposes for putting us on this earth in the Bible. It now becomes a question of how different people read and comprehend the Bible.

One thing is certain; however, there is only one Christian Bible. What Pastor Warren has done and done remarkably well was extract Bible verses, some out of context, and present them as God's purposes for our lives. That is his opinion of course, and he is entitled to it. The problem is he does not always point out that that is only his opinion. It is presented as fact.

The brilliance of Rick Warren's writings is of course his ability to surround an accurate statement with a bunch of unbiblical statements to make his point. Note in this instance that he correctly advises us to ask God if we want to know our true purpose. He also explains how this works. God answers us through His Word. He quotes Ephesian 1:11 to support his point but again spoils it all by giving us his own interpretation of the verse. He says, "You may choose your career, your spouse, your hobbies, and many other parts of your life, but you don't get to choose your purpose."

Really, Pastor, how can my purpose be different from all the things you have just enumerated that by definition constitute my life here on earth, i.e., what my God-centered and family rooted life is all about? If I do all these things right, and I have accepted Jesus and obey His commands, what is there to stop me from going to heaven? Last I checked, God only required that I live my life in obedience to Him. That is the only condition I need to satisfy in order to go to heaven, unless of course I have violated one of the other conditions with respect to forgiving those who trespass against us, blaspheming the Holy Spirit, and dying with unconfessed sins.

Why then, Pastor Warren, are you introducing a mystery where there should ordinarily be none?

The Pastor, at some point in this first chapter, finally tells us what his book is about. Oh wait for it! He says, "The purpose of your life fits into a much larger cosmic purpose that God has designed for eternity." Huh? What's that? He does not tell us what that cosmic stuff is about, which he says his book is about.

Whatever his book is about, that there is a foundational disconnect between what the book says on its cover, and what is actually between its covers is not in doubt. His five purposes follow.

THE PASTOR'S FIVE PURPOSES

The five purposes the Pastor tells us are God given, cleverly extracted from the Bible of course. However, are they valid? We are told:

We were planned for God's pleasure. This conjures up an image of those Roman emperors who built stadiums where gladiators fought each other to death for the emperor's pleasure.

We were formed for God's family. What about the Jew, the Muslim, and those who worship Buddha? Didn't God create them the same as the "born-again Christian"?

You were created to become like Christ. Yes, true. At creation, that is what God wanted, and there were no Jews and Gentiles then. There were no born-again Christians either—just Adam and Eve.

You were shaped for serving God. This idea is clearly exclusive to Pastor Warren, and the reader can embrace it if they so wish. It does not violate the scriptures.

You were made for a mission. Our whole sojourn on earth is a mission of course—a mission to live according to God's precepts. As long as we do that, we by definition do all the other good things the Pastor has enumerated.

NONBELIEVERS

It is also clear from the above purposes that the book, *The Purpose Driven Life*, is directed at that segment of God's human creations we identify as followers of Jesus Christ. By definition, believers do not include nonbelievers. This is another problem with the book. If you are going to talk about creation, i.e., we were created to be like Jesus, then that statement should apply to all of humanity and not just the segment that has accepted Jesus as Lord and Savior. After all, we are created equal in God's eyes. How, therefore, can we justify excluding two-thirds (non-Christians) of the human population and still be talking about creation?

Every time we talk about God's human creations [Adam and Eve], we are talking about all of humanity. Therefore, the focus on the reasons God gave for creating us in His own image and putting us on earth will necessarily apply to us all. It is true that God expects us to be like Him (Jesus) in terms of His nature.

One can understand why this mistaken view occurred. The Pastor must have been thinking God created us in His own image, logically, one can make the conclusion that He created us to be like Him. However, the parallel in our own lives should be instructive. Mom and Dad do not couple up to make a child just like "me." First of all, the variables are insurmountable. *Like me* for Mom is going to be different from *like me* for Dad. One would be planning (hoping) for a girl, while the other for a boy. One can accept that because God is perfect, He can create us to be like Himself, but because of our imperfections, we would hope our children are better than us, an improvement on us. That no parent ever sits there planning to have a child so it will be like themselves is obvious.

The Pastor has children, and I am sure he never sat there with his wife planning to have a child like himself. We all do expect them to be like the parents. It is a fine point to make, but it is important in underscoring the "disconnect" part in the Pastor's message.

That in the Pastor's mind, it is constantly reinforced in the the book that it is for believers only. In one section of the book, the author actually emphasizes service to other believers as opposed to service to mankind as a whole.

In the time of the Apostles, the context of such statements was clear. They were an endangered species and faced executions. It was important that they come to each other's aid. In the context of the "Parable of the Good Samaritan," Jesus was teaching that we are all the same in the eyes of our Creator. While one understands what Pastor Warren is trying to say, an approach to the human experience on earth that excludes all nonbelievers is unfortunate. Fortunately, most American mega churches with outreach programs abroad do not base their aid on the basis of that distinction. There are Christian groups that will aid only Jewish groups abroad, but there seem to be special considerations involved in these situations.

The bottom line is God put all humankind on this earth for the same reasons and for the same purpose(s). Unless I am mistaken, creation, according to the Bible, happened only once. That was when God created Adam and Eve.

We should always remember that even though the book's message is apparently about the born-again Christian, we are a minority. It is estimated that Christians make up roughly 32 percent of the world population. Given a world population of 7 billion, about a third of them or 2.2 billion are Christians. The scriptures do teach us however that the only way to the Father is through His son Jesus Christ. Translation: There must be a lot of lost souls out there according to the Christian doctrine, and if we accept that not all Christians will be saved, then the number that will ultimately dwell with the Lord for eternity becomes really small. This is of course a powerful weapon for Christian evangelism.

However, the point remains that the purposes(s) why God put us here on earth must necessarily deal with all 7 billion human beings because, as I have argued, those purposes were clearly spelled out in the Bible. They were to multiply and fill the earth, but Buddha's people and the Hindus have 22 percent, and Muslims add another 23 percent to make up half the world's population. Buddha, like all of humankind, believes in the same God—the One who created everything. The differences center on how we worship Him.

FINAL WORD ON ASKING GOD

How we communicate with God as Christians is not a mystery. By reading the Bible, we get to know what God has prescribed as acceptable or unacceptable behavior. Hearing and obeying His voice means knowing His Word on the subject at hand and applying it.

If a lustful Christian sets out to seduce someone not his wife and suddenly has doubts, that is the Holy Spirit tagging him and reminding him of the sin he is about to commit. A man of the world has no such doubts because he does not have a reference point for right or wrong in this area. He gleefully proceeds to conquer, and the conquered woman gleefully joins her counterpart in celebrating the new union.

The Christian, on the other hand, goes home full of remorse and goes on his knees and cries out to God asking for forgiveness. If the lustful Christian not only heard God's voice but also obeyed, the sin would not have been consummated.

You may ask, "How does this work again?" It's simple. You read in the Bible, and it says sex outside marriage is sinful. In disobedience, you go and have sex outside marriage. Because the Holy Spirit is in you and is a witness to your disobedience, all He does is remind you of God's directives on the subject. If you turn back from that temptation, you have *heard* the voice of God, *recognized* it. If you stop before committing the sin, you have *obeyed* His voice. That is Christianity made simple or *Christianity for Dummies.* If you do not read the Bible, these truths remain hidden from you.

Thus, one is either obedient or disobedient. Whether you know your true purpose as defined by the Pastor or not has no bearing on the question whether you will have everlasting life in heaven or not.

POINTS TO PONDER

Review Genesis 1:28.
Do you agree that God stated His reasons for creating mankind?
If He did, what are the implications on your responsibilities as a parent?

Scriptures: Genesis 1:28
               Genesis 9:18-29

CHAPTER 2

You Are Not an Accident

---

*We will learn in this chapter that we were planned by God;
therefore, we are not an accident. "God prescribed every single
detail of your body." He chose your race and color of your skin.
We are told because He made us, He has also decided when we
will be born and when we will die.*

Pastor Warren begins this chapter by reminding us that we are not an accident. God planned us long before we were conceived in our mother's womb. This is an accepted Christian doctrine. Yet, as one reads on, one starts to get the impression that we are dealing with elements of predestination in some of the things Pastor Rick Warren has to say in this chapter.

He, however, avoids being bogged down by not stating one way or the other whether he believes in predestination. Given the controversies that often accompany any meaningful discussion of biblical predestination, he probably was wise in doing so.

We cannot, however, overlook allusions to God's foreknowledge of us, determining who our parents would be, what color of skin we would be, where we would be born, and where we would live. The Pastor is saying we were predestined to be who we are today. That leads people to ask questions. One of those questions is if God already knows my fate (destiny), i.e., my fate is sealed, what is the point of going to church, praying, and doing all the good things the scriptures say I should do if it will have no bearing on my destiny?

A more troubling question by saints is if God planned it all, and God is love, how do we explain children who are born with birth defects? Is it all planned by God, or is the devil responsible for these disastrous situations? We know we cannot carry on this discussion without factoring in the activities of the devil. We know Satan's goal is to oppose everything God plans. Is it possible that if God planned us, and God is love and only does good and not evil, then the devil was allowed to have his way in these situations?

That, of course, begs this question, "Under what circumstances does God allow Satan into our lives?" These issues unfortunately come up a lot in our churches, and when a man of the cloth makes statements like the ones Pastor Warren makes in this chapter, the saints are entitled to ask.

This discourse, therefore, needed to be accompanied by an explanation why, if God planned it all, bad things continue to happen even to believers. Asking these questions does not mean I can make a convincing argument that the devil did it all either. That would be to accord him too much power. However, like many things concerning God, the real answer might be we do not really know the real answer.

It is a fact that God, in His infinite wisdom, has never revealed the exact interplay between Himself and Satan. The scriptures reveal part of this relationship.[18] We know from the Bible that Satan was welcome to join in when God met with His sons. As far as we know, that relationship remained the same, at least until the death of Christ. At that point, we are told by the Lord Jesus Himself that *"Now is the time for judgment on this world; now the prince of this world will be driven out. And I, when I am lifted up from the earth, will draw all people to myself."*[19]

From this passage, we have reasons to believe that the devil was kicked out of heaven and now no longer has the privilege of attending meetings when God meets with His sons. Two things are not revealed here however: (1) Who are God's sons? (2) Is Satan one of them? Such references to God's sons in the Bible may have contributed to cults, such as the Mormons, believing that, in addition to Jesus, God had other sons including Lucifer. It is noteworthy that Revelation, the last canon of the

---

[18] Job 1:6
[19] John 12:31-32

Bible to be written, confirms that Satan still lives on earth, and his role is still the same. Then again, hopefully, he is no longer able to attend God's meetings in heaven.

The Bible reveals another part of the nature of the relationship between God and the devil. God revealed that Satan cannot attack a righteous man without His permission.[20] Christians generalize this to mean Satan cannot attack a believer without God's permission. We automatically equate a believer to a righteous man, but are we correct in doing so? Be warned, therefore, that we might be completely wrong on this. Job was a righteous person. By contrast, the Bible tells us we are sinful people. The devil might already have license to attack us due to our sinful nature. (We are not righteous people.)

Remember also that, when we sin, we give Satan a foothold into our lives.[21] If I am right, then Satan can attack a sinner at will. That can easily explain the children born with defects, world disasters, and all these bad things that happen to good people, so to speak.

PREDESTINATION AND SALVATION

If I am destined to be saved, what difference will my personal efforts at salvation make? It does not take much for one to realize that the idea that everything about our lives was preplanned by God contradicts the equally plausible idea that God allows us to choose between righteousness and evil. If we accept the proposition that everything about us has already been predetermined, aren't we making a mockery of the scriptures that say otherwise?

For example, we learn from the Bible that *"There is no difference between the Jew and the Greek: for the same Lord over all is rich unto all that call upon him. For whosoever shall call upon the name of the Lord shall be saved."*[22] This sounds like an open invitation for all unsaved souls to repent and be saved. It calls on people, saved or unsaved, to call on the Lord regardless of whether they are Jews or Gentiles. Yet Pastor Rick

---

[20] Job 1:7-12

[21] Ephesians 4:26-27

[22] Romans 10:12-13

Warren, by not approaching the subject directly to avoid controversy, left many unanswered questions by what he had to say in this chapter.

Of course, he can also argue that God knew you would someday turn around, repent, and be saved. That becomes a circular argument without an exit, and we will avoid that here. His point was to state the widely accepted truth that God is all knowing, without dealing with the related questions. For example, one might ask, if God is all knowing and has planned every day of my life, how come He has allowed so much suffering to take place in my life?

Do not misunderstand me. There is also truth in the proposition that God knows all about you and me even before we were born. However, there are different degrees of knowledge. There is merit in saying that God has the capability to know, but for other reasons, He might choose not to know just as He allows us to choose, even if the choices we make are the wrong ones. That would also explain why disasters happen or tragedies happen that are sometimes quickly reversed through prayer.

We are all too aware of situations where doctors are going to operate on someone who has been badly injured, and all of a sudden the prognosis changes, and the doctors report that the person is recovering on their own after the family and church have prayed for divine intervention.

The truth is these are God's miracles, and we should not always try to find answers because there are usually no answers. God does as God does. He is both sovereign and unfathomable. Everything is possible with Him. It is, therefore, entirely possible that, for the people God wants to use, He might choose to know a lot more about them than the people He has no special use for. For these chosen few, He might order their every step from the moment they are conceived in their mother's womb for example, while for you and me, He might simply let nature take its course.

We know that God uses everybody in different ways, but for a select few, He has special uses for them. If God knew that Barrack Obama was going to be the leader of the so-called free world one day, He might indeed have ordered Obama's every step from the day he was conceived in his mother's womb to the day he became President of the United States. Then again, did God order every step of that "wino" now feeding out of garbage cans in downtown Manhattan?

We see in Moses the way God prepared him for the role he had planned for him. Moses needed to be born a Jew, and he was. He needed to be raised a Pharaoh, and he was. He needed to be tested, and he was.

By the same token, statements made by God to His especially chosen people might, therefore, be specific to those people. Things God said to Moses, David, Elijah, Elisha, and others might, therefore, not have universal application to you and me. The caveat here is we just do not know for certain, and chances are we will never know.

There are people in this world who are born with special gifts. Some of them begin to prophesy at an early age. We also know from direct observation that the majority of us are just common ordinary folk. We are people of average intelligence, and we kind of get by in life. There is nothing very special about us.

Then again, if you have lived in our day and age, you are no doubt aware of a certain Michael Jackson who could mesmerize the world by his music and dance. Was he destined? Where did all that talent come from, and why was it given only to Michael and not to anyone else? None of his siblings has even come close to duplicating his talent.

We learn from the scripture, for example, that *"many are called but few are chosen."*[23] Could this be applied to the Michael Jackson story? The truth is we can speculate all we want, but we do not know, and we will never know the exact answer. We, however, assume that we know exactly what that verse in the Bible means, but do we?

More often than not, we do not understand the real meaning of such a verse, and chances are we will never know. As Christians, we need to accept that God is a mystery and that we try to demystify Him for our own purposes. There are areas of Him and about Him He has chosen to keep hidden from us. In real life, different people tackle the verse and try to give it meaning, but many stumble in the effort.

I first heard about the verse "many are called but few are chosen" from my mother, and she gave it its religious significance. She applied it to men of the cloth who achieved greatness. These were people God had chosen to do special things on this earth. For example, many people are qualified to be the pope in Rome, but only a few ever make it. That is the meaning my mother gave that verse, and that is the meaning I choose to give it too.

We can apply the verse to other areas of life of course. For example, many Christians have tried to write a religious treatise that will influence the world, but Rick Warren and a few others have actually managed

---

[23]   Matthew 22:1-14

to do it. These are the chosen few according to my mother. The called are all those that have tried. For the presidency of the United States, many have tried, but only a few have succeeded. Barack Obama, George Bush, and George Bush again, Bill Clinton—all the way back to George Washington—have succeeded where many have tried and failed. If we accept that "rulership" is God ordained, then we must also accept my mother's view of the verse.

Today's Christian leaders have settled for an interpretation that says God has invited everyone to be saved, but only a few will actually be saved. Ouch! That's a downer. At least give us some hope! I personally believe it means we are all invited to serve Him, but few will be chosen to actually serve Him in the special manner of a high priest, a prophet or an apostle.

Likewise, the idea that God might have chosen slavery for some even before they were born and royalty for others is hard to digest. We first see an allusion to this possibility in the scriptures with respect to Noah cursing his youngest son Ham.[24] It is not clear what Ham's crime was. The Bible simply tells us he saw his father in a drunken stupor and naked. He told his brothers who then covered Noah up without looking at his nakedness. It is said when Noah found out what Ham had done to him, he then cursed him. The actual verse says, *"When Noah awoke from his wine and found out what his youngest son had done to him, he said Cursed be Canaan! The lowest of slaves will he be to his brothers."*[25] Canaan was Ham's son. So much for sins of the father!

The above verse leaves more to the imagination, much like the one referencing Adam and Eve's forbidden fruit. God deliberately withholds detail where detail will not add much to His message. These are the elements of God's mystery, and it is pointless trying to find out more, for all we end up doing is speculating about what must have really happened.

It is worthy of remembering that, in Hebrews, we are told that *"Jesus Christ is the same yesterday and today and forever."*[26] Yet to our human eyes, the personified God in Jesus Christ appears to be a more forgiving, kinder, and compassionate God than the one who led Moses and the Jews out of bondage in Egypt—the God who ordered the wanton destruction

---

[24] Genesis 9:24
[25] Genesis 9:24-25
[26] Hebrews 13:8

of people so His chosen people could have a home in Israel. He is a far cry from the God personified in the new covenant. However, the verse that He is the yesterday, forever, remains true because He told us so.

Yes, He is the same God.

One only needs to read the Book of Joshua and some of the Old Testament scriptures to suspect that the new covenant with Jesus is almost devoid of violence, murder, and mass killings in the name of God. This is especially true for Christians than it is for some of the other non-Christian religions. We still have other faiths that adhere to the belief that mass murder in the name of our Creator is justified, and some of the Old Testament stories can be used to support that belief.

In a way, when we drop bombs on the innocent and defenseless to rid the world of Saddam Hussein, we may explain it away by using the Old Testament and today's political imperatives. The New Testament, however, seems to preach a different type of love that rarely countenances the loss of life.

Coming back to our argument, we know for example that God does not use everyone the same way He used His prophets like Isaiah, Elijah, and Elisha. These were people He especially chose to be His prophets, so there is no denying that God chooses some people for His special purposes. It is possible that, He knows most of us all right. However, since He has no special plans for us beyond being fruitful, multiplying and populating the earth and taking dominion over His other creations, He does not focus that much on us but just let's nature take its course. Now before you throw a thousand verses that contradict what I am saying, let me admit that I am aware of them, and that is part of the problem I am addressing. Don't try and defrock God. Hallelujah!

The issue of predestination remains a troubling one. It stands in stark contradiction to Bible verses that invite us to repent and be baptized. If predestination is as defined, what would be the point of that effort if our fate was already sealed before we were even born? Remember the scripture that says, *"Repent, therefore, and turn around so as to get your sins blotted out, that seasons of refreshing may come from the person of Jehovah."*[27]

Ezekiel says much the same thing. He says, *"But if a wicked person turns away from all the sins they have committed and keeps all my decrees and does what is just and right, that person will surely live; they will not die.*

---

[27]   Acts 3:19

None of the offenses they have committed will be remembered against them. Because of the righteous things they have done, they will live. Do I take any pleasure in the death of the wicked? declares the Sovereign LORD. *Rather, am I not pleased when they turn from their ways and live?"*[28]

It is difficult to reconcile predestination with these two passages from the Bible.

POINTS TO PONDER

If God planned me and everybody else born into the human species, how do we explain children born with defects?

When a child is born with defects, is God disciplining the parents by letting them go through trials and tribulations, or is the devil in charge?

Scriptures: Job 1:6-8
                 Ezekiel 18:21-23

---

[28]   Ezekiel 18:21-23

CHAPTER 3

What Drives Your Life

The basic teaching in this chapter is that "everyone's life is driven by something." Pastor Warren tells us that some of us are driven by guilt, by resentment and anger, by fear, by materialism, and by the need for approval. The Pastor tells us that the benefits of a purpose driven life include the fact that knowing our purpose (1) gives meaning to our lives, (2) simplifies our lives, (3) focuses our lives, (4) motivates our lives, and (5) prepares us for eternity.

This is another chapter where there is very little one can disagree with the Pastor. Everyone's life is indeed driven by something, and literally speaking, each one of us thinks they know precisely what drives us.

There are four things all of us would like to have in our lives that could also be bad drivers if allowed into the driver's seat of our lives. We are told so because these guys can also be bad drivers. They are (1) possessions or greed, (2) popularity, (3) power, and (4) position. We all would love to have these four things, but be forewarned that they can easily develop into idols.

Pastor Warren in his book lists guilt, resentment and anger, fear, materialism, and need for approval as being among the things that can drive our lives. He says, however, that the more important drivers of one's life are those related to our mission here on earth as believers.

Before delving deeper into what the Pastor has to say on this subject, let us look elsewhere for ideas with respect to our purposes here on earth. We should be careful to restate that God's purposes for us on earth are explicitly stated in Genesis 1:28. What we are about to identify are our purposes for connecting with God. 1 Chronicles 28 deals with King David's imparting words of wisdom to his son, later to become King Solomon. The emphasis here was on connecting with God. Pastor Warren fails to make the important distinction that, when we begin life, we do not begin it as believers. That life, influenced as it is by the spirit of the world, continues until we become believers by being born again. When we are born again, a new and additional dimension is added to our lives; but depending on where we are on the human life cycle chart, our purposes and drivers do not change. We might need to make some adjustments here and there to conform our lives to a Christian lifestyle however. If Oprah, who is criticized by some Pentecostals for her new-age religion views were to be born again (again), I doubt the purposes and drivers in her life would change that much.

This observation alone serves to bring the statement by Pastor Warren that the more important drivers of our lives are those that relate to our mission here on earth as believers into question.

The issue is to establish what it is that comes into play when we are born again. We know we are required to develop good spiritual habits going forward. Had Pastor Warren recognized the unity of life, he would have avoided any tension between the true purpose(s) why God put us here and our purposes in quest for eternity (the God connection). This approach aligns perfectly with my creation approach (Genesis 1:28) to answering the original question "What on earth am I here for?" In our quest for eternity, our purposes are as follows:

> *Purpose No. 1* is to connect with God personally. Your personal walk with God is anchored in your life—the life you are living right now.

> *Purpose No. 2* is to commit to God's church. This is a no-brainer because the church is the only organization God left behind on earth. How can you, therefore, effectively connect with God without a church connection?

Purpose No. 3 is to cultivate spiritual habits. We are talking here about Christianity being a lifestyle. The "Parable of the Sower" tells us our heart field has four types of soil—the road side, the rocky place, the thorny (weeds) ground, and the fertile ground. Cultivating spiritual habits is akin to cultivating our heart field until we remove all the rocks, the hard places (roadside), and thorns so that it will become a fertile ground ready to receive the Word of God (the seed) to take root in us.

Purpose No. 4 is to care for God's people. The Bible gives us a good example of what we are talking about here when it says, *"All the believers were together and had everything in common. Selling their possessions and goods, they gave to anyone as he had need. Every day they continued to meet together in the temple courts. They broke bread in their homes and ate together with glad and sincere hearts, praising God and enjoying the favor of all the people. And the Lord added to their number daily those who were being saved."*[29]

Purpose No. 5 is to celebrate God's work. We do that through worship.

Pastor Warren says the most important drivers of our lives are those that relate to our mission here on earth. He states that mission in terms of his five purposes for a purpose driven life. What emerges from his discourse is that our mission here on earth is seeking everlasting life in heaven. I think he is wrong in this analysis because that deals only with our spiritual lives—the God connection.

Our lives here on earth constitute what God calls a lifetime. That life with its purposes and drivers comes first. That is the life we are born into. At some point in our lives, we make the decision to accept Jesus as our Lord and Savior. We are born again. It is at that point that we begin our walk with Jesus. It is also the point our quest for eternity begins.

According to Pastor Warren, it is at that point in life that what he calls our mission on earth as believers begins, which is true. However,

---

[29] Acts 2:42-47

for many people, they do not turn to Jesus until they are in their teens, twenties, thirties, forties, fifties, etc. We are not going to argue that these people's lives had no meaning or important drivers or whatsoever until then, are we?

It would appear that, for many people, their purposes and the things that drive their lives are well established at the point they begin their walk with Jesus. Those purposes and the things that drive our lives do not change but might need to be modified to conform them to a Christian lifestyle. The extent of the changes to be made depends on how much of a sinner one was before being born again.

Pastor Warren's approach begs a number of questions as follows:

(1) What is really our mission on earth?

(2) Why should life's drivers related to our mission here on earth be different from those related to our day-to-day lives?

If taking care of our households qualifies us as believers (1 Timothy 5:8), isn't it true then that failure to satisfy that threshold requirement disqualifies us as believers even if we are born again?

POINTS TO PONDER

We all like power, possession, position, and popularity. What role do these things play in your life?

How can you ensure that they do not become idols?

In our quest for eternity, do you agree that our lives need to be conformed to a Christian lifestyle?

How should we go about doing that?

In God's eyes, what do you think our mission here on earth is?

Scripture: 1 Chronicles 28
               1 Timothy 5:8
               Acts 2:42-47

CHAPTER 4

Defining Our Mission On Earth

(Warren's Day 3 Cont'd)

The Pastor tells us about our mission here on earth as believers but does not define it for us. The chapter examines that aspect of his message.

Our mission on earth as a species has already been defined for us by our Creator, and as we have seen, it is anchored in Genesis 1.28. We learned here that it is to be fruitful and multiply. It is to fill the earth and subdue it. It is to take dominion of God's other creations. When so defined in terms of what God actually said and did when He created us, we can derive from there the elements that will drive our daily lives, and one of them is taking care of our households.

Our mission as Christians has to be anchored within that framework—the framework of the lives we live in accordance with God's overall design. The analysis should take the form of (1) if we are to multiply, what should we be doing to accomplish that purpose? Since this involves having children, a man clearly needs to (2) find a wife, and we know God created them man and woman for this purpose. Adam's wife was delivered from his rib, but for his descendants (us), we have to look for one. To get one, we need to (3) pursue and win her love. To woe and win her love, we have to demonstrate to her (4) our potential to succeed in order to support her and our children and so on.

Each of these steps has its own purpose and driver. For example, to establish oneself as husband material, one has to show and demonstrate promise (potential). Girls are known for refusing to marry vagabonds, if given a choice.

If we go back to our human life cycle chart, we can see that the process of establishing ourselves is a long and drawn-out process that starts early in life. From the moment we are born, we are preparing for this big step. In our modern day, we go to school, we go to college, or we learn a trade, get a job, and the like as part of our preparation.

As our consciousness about ourselves increases with age, we start to talk and think about who we might marry. Most of these things are done instinctively because they are programmed into our DNA. The child thinks this way because it is in his/her nature, and at the appropriate age, they will actually do just as God instructed.

A thirteen-year-old on average if asked about marriage will tell you they are too young to marry. It is the same DNA instruction, however, that tells the same thirteen-year-old to date a member of the opposite sex. We do not teach our children these things because they are already written into their DNA. Yet God made us so by the time we reach puberty, we are fully equipped biologically to pair off and start our own families. Culture then intervenes, especially in the western world to tell the child "You cannot marry yet. You are still too young to assume the responsibilities and obligations of a parent." Parents recognize that being biologically ready is not the same thing as being mentally and emotionally prepared for that big step.

There are still cultures out there, however, that obey that natural clock and allow girls to be married off at fourteen or younger. Most cultures today recognize that, at that age, a child is still growing physically, mentally, and emotionally and therefore not ready for the responsibilities of marriage.

Now if we asked the same thirteen-year-old the same question about marriage a mere ten years later, the answer that we will get will be very different. It will either be I am already married, I am already married with children, or I am preparing to get married. Some might say they are in the process of looking for Mr. Right or Ms. Right. Yet others might have chosen to delay the process for career reasons, as is typically the case with children who go on to medical school, law school, and graduate school.

There is another group too, a minority in our day and age, that might have already decided that they do not want to marry or have children. This group is the exception rather than the rule. We need not concern ourselves here with them.

The point is that this development to maturity has already been programmed into us by our Creator and is reinforced by what we see around us from the moment we are born. We see a Mom and a Dad, a man and a woman, nurturing us and a vague notion develops that, when we grow up, we will do the same. This part of us is instinctual, and we see it in other species God has created as well. The mating game is universal.

What drives us through all these early stages of development is partly natural and partly imposed by parents whose job is to prepare us for the future. Part of it is learned from observing life around us. The most significant of these influences is the parental instruction for us to go to school. Children cannot initially appreciate the significance of school until they are old enough to understand. Slowly, they learn that they are required to accomplish certain things like learning the ABCs and learning to count. Later, they learn they are required to pass tests, get good grades, etc. It is a process, and as time goes on, the child begins to take ownership of the process. The goals of the parent for the child begin to transfer to the child during the growing up process.

Most of this comes to us naturally as part of our growth, but as the Pastor correctly said the need for approval can also be a significant driver at this stage as well. It is also true that, on a balance, a child driven by anger tends to be destructive. They are constantly aggravating those around them, especially in the home. The children driven by love, on the other hand, tend to be constructive and seek to please those around them, including their parents and teachers.

We learn at an early age what is expected of us in all areas of our lives. The parent says to the child, "Hang up your jacket," "Make up your bed," "Clean up your room," "Pick up after yourself," etc. as part of the training needed for junior with little thought what they (the parent) are doing.

The other purposes in our lives are fulfilled by other things we do, sometimes things out of our control. The desire to succeed is not always something we control entirely for example. One can be born into a society where there are no schools for example. Others are born into strife because of the many civil wars we have witnessed that cause a whole generation to be lost. The Eastern Congo has known no peace for a very long time. We can summarize this by saying the circumstances of one's birth can influence the rest of their life.

There is, therefore, so much to life—the purpose of life and what drives our lives that we cannot reduce it to a formula for living.

THEREFORE, HOW DO WE ANSWER THE PASTOR'S QUESTION?

First, we need to identify the "disconnect" in the Pastor's reasoning. If you live in America, God gave you this life. The one you are experiencing right now with your wife, Sally, or your husband, Hubert, with your two and a half kids and the dog. That is the life you need to use to make a difference for you for eternity. Every detail in this life contributes to the final judgment whether you go to heaven or hell. The abstract context of some parts of Pastor Warren's book only serve to obscure that truth.

The answer is you should (1) connect personally with God, (2) commit to a church (go to church), (3) cultivate spiritual habits, (4) care for God's people (love thy neighbor), and (5) celebrate God's work in you. The life you lead does not change but is conformed to a Christian lifestyle by cultivating spiritual habits.

Notice the difference. You do not need to "pause" your everyday life to do the things the Pastor says you need to do for eternity. You only need to conform your very life, its purposes and drivers, to what God demands of you by developing spiritual habits and by living a Christian lifestyle.

To understand how Pastor Warren might have gotten his purposes wrong, therefore, one needs to look at the Great Commission, which was given by Jesus Christ to His disciples just before He ascended to heaven. He said to them, *"All authority in heaven and on earth has been given to me. Therefore go and make disciples of all nations, baptizing them in the name of the Father and of the Son and of the Holy Spirit, and teaching them to obey everything I have commanded you. And surely I am with you always, to the very end of the age."*[30] In as far as baptism by water and the Holy

---

[30]   Matthew 28:16-20

Spirit marks the beginning of our walk with Christ, his book begins. However, in planning and designing his book, he failed to articulate this; he did not take our present lives in tow with him.

A lot of what Pastor Warren says in his book appears inspired by this scripture. If we take the Great Commission as the beginning of our spiritual walk with Christ, then the context of what Pastor Warren is saying begins to make some sense. The people who are engaged in preaching the Word as a vocation might indeed have their lives driven by a greater purpose, which includes a Jesus-like lifestyle and going around the world spreading the Good News.

A number of our religious leaders are already doing this as we speak. Tune into the Church Channel, and one can see what these people are doing around the globe. They even discovered "black" Jews in Zimbabwe.

However, the average Joe's life remains the same except for the fact that the things that are not pleasing to God have to be weeded out. Even for the men and women of the cloth, their lives remain firmly anchored in family, and the life cycle chart events in their personal lives are very much a part of it.

While people like to say "You can't take it (your possessions) with you when you die," God wants you to pass it on to your children. You have earned it. He says a good man leaves an inheritance for his children and children's children.[31] We see that all the time in real life. Paul Crouch, the visionary behind the Trinity Broadcasting Network, was very much a family man. Even if he apparently died without a will, the empire he built like the Rockefellers and the Fords before him, goes to his children. It is biblical.

Speaking of family as the basic unit of a Christian lifestyle, Benny Hinn realized the emptiness of success without a wife and went back to his wife. That clearly made him whole again. Spreading the Good News and healing people in the name of Jesus Christ now has more meaning again for him.

However, postulating that the ordinary believer's life, driven as it is by the need to support a family, has as its primary driver a higher purpose is unrealistic and impractical. A more accurate view is one that sees our quest for eternity as superimposed over our ordinary lives. The higher goals the Pastor talks about are a mere reflection of the quality of the lives

---

[31] Proverbs 13:22

we actually live in Jesus's terms. If we fail to meet the basic threshold of caring for our households, we are unlikely to enter the Kingdom of God anyway.[32] Therefore, your reflection in the mirror cannot be more than the substance of the real person you see in it. What should be important for every Christian is what we need to do to qualify for eternity. Our focus should be on the essential building blocks that will get us there. Those building blocks are the little things we do from the moment we wake up to the moment we go back to bed. It has nothing to do with knowing our purposes why we are here on earth. God requires only that our lives, as driven as they are by a multiplicity of factors and events, including as the Pastor correctly says, fear, anger, the need for approval, keeping up with the Joneses, need to pay the bills, etc., should remain God centered.

The Pastor, in this respect, failed to properly anchor his question "What drives our lives" in our reality. In doing so, he introduced a certain degree of confusion into the subject. The real question should have been "What drives our lives in our quest for eternity?" In other words, our lives are intact, but now we seek a personal connection with God. What therefore should we change, modify, or eliminate so we can enjoy full fellowship with the Almighty God?

Another argument that can be used to expose the errors in Pastor Warren's thinking on the issue of what drives our lives is the fact that Christianity is a lifestyle. That means everything we do, we do in obedience to God. There is no separation between what we do for God and what we do for ourselves for it is the same life we are serving.

The idea is to conform everything we do so it pleases our Maker. We are required to conform our lifestyles, not to the influences of this world even as we live in it. The scripture says, *"Do not conform to the pattern of this world, but be transformed by the renewing of your mind. Then you will be able to test and approve what God's will is—his good, pleasing and perfect will."*[33]

This teaching does not call for us to abandon what we do in every area of our lives in order to qualify for the Kingdom of God. It simply tells us to conform that which we do to what God expects of us which

---

[32]   1 Timothy 5:8
[33]   Romans 12:2

means to live our lives in obedience to the Almighty. What we do on a day-to-day basis cannot therefore be divorced from our quest for eternity.

The Bible says if you fail to meet your primary responsibilities as a parent, you have denied the faith, and you are worse than an unbeliever. The actual passage teaches us that *"Anyone who does not provide for their relatives, and especially for their own household, has denied the faith and is worse than an unbeliever."*[34] This scripture provides authoritative affirmation, that is, fulfilling our basic responsibilities as parents, we are also making a down payment towards everlasting life. Moreover, providing for our families is what we do. That is the one sure driver for the great majority of mankind.

POINTS TO PONDER

What drives your life?
Where are you on the Life Cycle Chart?
Are you on track?
There should be no separation between what drives your life and what drives your quest for eternity. Do you agree? Why or why not?
Christianity is a lifestyle. What does that mean to you?
There can be some bad drivers in the driver's seat of your life. What are they?
There is nothing wrong with having possessions, popularity, power, and position; but these should not drive your life. Do you agree? Why or why not?

Scriptures: 1 Chronicles 28 (Connecting with God)
               Matthew 18:20 (Fellowship)
               Hebrews 10:25

---

[34]   1 Timothy 5:8

28

CHAPTER 5

Knowing Our Purpose

(Warren's Day 3 Cont'd)

We will explore in this chapter the idea that knowing our purpose (1) gives meaning to our lives, (2) simplifies our lives, (3) focuses our lives, (4) motivates our lives, and (5) prepares us for eternity.

Pastor Rick Warren says knowing our purpose(s) in life gives meaning to our lives, but given that the purposes he offers are rather abstract, it is difficult to translate this into everyday life experiences. We need a bridge to move us forward.

I have argued that our purposes on earth are God given. They are explicitly stated in the Bible, and they are to be fruitful and multiply. To be fruitful and to multiply means to procreate. By definition, this means a man and a woman come together and become one flesh and start a family.

Gill's Exposition of the whole Bible says about Genesis 1:28, "And God said unto them [Adam and Eve], be fruitful, and multiply, and replenish the earth: if this is not an express command, as the Jews understand it, for marriage and procreation of children, it seems to be more than a bare permission; at least it is a direction and an advice to what was proper and convenient for the increase of mankind, and for the filling of the earth with inhabitants, which was the end of its being made."

Gill's Exposition continues by citing the Bible when it says, *"For this is what the LORD says he who created the heavens, he is God; he who fashioned and made the earth, he founded it; he did not create it to be empty, but formed it to be inhabited he says I am the LORD, and there is no other."*[35]

The above passages do a good job of defining for us what God must have meant by the words *be fruitful, multiply,* and *fill the earth and take dominion of my other creations.* There was also a mention in there (Gill's) about marriage, and we know from scripture that no one is allowed to have children out of wedlock. That tells us that marriage has always been part of God's plan for mankind.

Scriptures tell us something about marriage: *"He answered, "Have you not read that he who created them from the beginning made them male and female, and said, 'Therefore a man shall leave his father and his mother and hold fast to his wife, and the two shall become one flesh'? So they are no longer two but one flesh. What therefore God has joined together let not man separate [put asunder."*[36]

Gill's Whole Bible Exposition also comments on the phrase "subdue it." It says, *"And subdue it; the earth; not that it was in the hands of others, who had no right to it, and to be conquered and taken out of their hands; but is to be understood of their taking possession, and making use of it; of their tilling the land, and making it subservient to their use."*[37]

Wikipedia gives us another perspective on procreation and the biological imperatives and reproduction that are involved. "In order for species to persist, they must by definition reproduce to ensure the continuation of their species. Without reproduction the species ceases to exist. The capacity for reproduction and the drive to do so whenever physiological and environmental conditions allow it are universal among living organisms and are expressed in a multitude of ways by the spectrum of living organisms."

The instruction to multiply is programmed so deeply into our DNA that we obey it instinctively. The whole animal world does too. Only a few people have managed to disregard the parenting instinct completely. Depending on how one defines our mission on earth, most people I know believe they know their purpose in this life, even though some only have

---

[35] Isaiah 45:18

[36] Matthew 19:4-6

[37] Genesis 1:28

a vague idea what that purpose is. It is not something we actually write down on paper, but it is something we believe we know. Even if one thinks their purpose is to live (as opposed to dying), as their life unfolds, they will know their purpose. It goes something like this:

> Go to school, get good grades, go to college, get good grades, get a good job that pays, find an apartment away from Mom and Dad (there are exceptions), get a boyfriend/girlfriend, if you do not already have one etc. Note this character is approaching parenthood even though it is still just a vague idea. Get married and have children.

As the child matures, he/she begins to take ownership of his/her own destiny, step-by-step, until at twenty-three (United States) or thereabouts when they take full control. Thereafter, the basic character of this individual finds expression in how well he/she handles both career and family responsibilities and obligations and grows spiritually. Even for children still living with their parents, they have chores and other responsibilities to fulfill, and they know or should know what those chores are.

The bottom line is that, even though most of us do not reduce our purposes for living to pen and paper, we are nonetheless conscious of them. We, therefore, need to reject Pastor Warren's idea that we do not know our purpose for being here on earth.

KNOWING YOUR PURPOSE GIVES MEANING TO LIFE

The Pastor says that knowing our purpose gives meaning to life. The implication here being that people who do not know their purpose in life (in the spiritual sense) live lives that have no meaning.

Well, I can show Pastor Warren quite a few of my Jewish friends that are not (Christian) believers who lead very meaningful lives—lives that manifest the fruit of the spirit. There is love, joy, peace, forbearance, kindness, goodness, faithfulness, gentleness, and self-control in their lives. Some are also very rich people in the sense of Abraham, Job, and Solomon to boot.

I can also point to a number of Muslims and Buddhist friends who are leading very meaningful lives as well. They are also leaving very holy lives, and if perchance they do not make it to heaven, it will be not because of their misdeeds, but simply because they have not accepted Jesus as their Lord and Savior.

Jesus is quoted as saying, *"I am the way and the truth and the life. No one comes to the Father except through me."*[38] Apostle Paul caps it off by saying, *"If you declare with your mouth, 'Jesus is Lord,' and believe in your heart that God raised him from the dead, you will be saved."*[39]

It is clear from the above that by failing to define for us what he meant by life has no meaning, he left us hanging because, as I have pointed out, we all know people who are not believers who live meaningful lives by our human eyes. Hence, a person, by defining things to suit their message, is able to make his/her point. Pastor Warren was able to create the illusion that the things that drive our Christian lives are different from those that drive our everyday lives. He has convinced many of us that our mission on earth is other than what God said it ought to be according to Genesis 1:28.

My advice to believers and nonbelievers alike is that, whatever you do, do not let death remove you from this earth without accepting Jesus as your Lord and Savior. You die with unconfessed sin, and you are setting yourself up for damnation. Cover all bases even if you do not believe deep down that the Jesus's story is the real deal. If you are right, you have nothing to lose. If you are wrong, you fry in hell forever.

KNOWING OUR PURPOSE SIMPLIFIES OUR LIVES

We can accept this proposition that knowing our purpose simplifies our lives in the sense that it gives us a roadmap to the future. Smart parents with the means have education funds set aside for their children's education. For parents who do not have these programs in place, it is usually because they lack the means. They are struggling to make ends meet as it is, and therefore, the family budget leaves no room for these extras.

---

[38]   John 14:6
[39]   Romans 10:9

Clearly, the proposition that knowing our purpose in life can simplify our lives is acceptable, just as having a family budget accomplishes the same goals. By the same token, knowing our purpose *focuses* and *motivates* our lives. It does not "**prepare us for eternity**" as the Pastor claims. One who lives his life in obedience to God even if he has no clue what his purpose on earth is will most likely enter the Kingdom of God on the basis of what the Bible tells us. The eternity part of our lives depends entirely on doing God's will and not on just knowing it. That means you can know your purpose, but if you live in disobedience, which does nothing for your quest for eternity, you won't get there.

Of course, some of us take our chances by believing that, as long as we are under the cross, our sins are washed away (forgiven). Some pastors go to the extent of teaching that, when you are under the cross, it's like standing under a faucet or a shower. Any dirt (sin) that lands on you is automatically washed away. But there has to be a point where God's grace stops because of repeated sin. God regards continually sinning as tantamount to rejecting Jesus, which others argue is blasphemy.

SUCCESS AND FAILURE AS INDICATORS OF GOD'S PLAN AND WILL FOR US

Given the reality that God will not tell us in clear enough terms what our purpose on earth is, we can have a reasonable idea what His will and plan for us might be in another way. All humanity shares one thing in common, and that is our constant striving for success. When we succeed in whatever we do, we have reason to believe that both God's will and His purpose (plan) for our lives have been fulfilled.

We react differently when we fail. We harbor a suspicion that maybe it was not God's will for us to do whatever we did and failed, or that because of our sins, we allowed Satan (the Enemy) a foothold into our lives. As a consequence, he has engineered our failure. After all, the devil's mission is to steal, kill, and destroy. He steals our blessings if we give him a foothold. We, of course, pray that the situation be turned around by divine intervention.

This separation between our reality and what the Pastor says should be our reality is a foundational disconnect for his teaching and needs to be revisited. The most significant drivers in our lives are necessarily related to the need to support our families, and that is biblical.

POINTS TO PONDER

Do you know your purpose?
How does knowing your purpose help you in your personal walk with Christ?
Are You Married?
Are you happy?
What can you do to bring more joy into your life to get back on track?
(Note that divorce is not always the answer.)

Scriptures: John 14:6
                Isaiah 45:18

CHAPTER 6

Made to Last Forever

(Warren's Day 4)

We will learn in this chapter that we have an inborn instinct that longs for immortality. Even though our earthly bodies die, it is not the end. God wired our brains for immortality, and that is why we fail to accept the reality of death. Life, however, transcends the here and now. There is another life waiting for us after we leave this earth and that life offers only two options: heaven or hell. God has a purpose for you on earth, but it does not end here. We need to grasp the truth that life on earth is a preparation for eternity, and when we do, we will choose to live differently.

The statement that we are made to last forever is at first glance misleading. The Bible is clear that we have a lifetime on earth; therefore, we are not made to last forever. The Pastor makes this statement because, in the context of his book, life on earth and the afterlife are treated as one.

We do know our bodies die and are returned to earth (dust). When he says we are made to last forever, he is not talking about our earthly bodies which die, and the Bible confirms it. In this chapter, he quotes a verse from Ecclesiastes that says God *"has made everything beautiful in its time. He has also set eternity in the human heart; yet no one can fathom what God has done from beginning to end."*[40] From this, the Pastor makes the conclusion that this is what gives us a desire to live forever.

The conclusion is in line with conventional Christian doctrine that is based on this biblical truth. There are verses in the Bible that suggest that this belief, though biblically true, might not be the whole truth. Biblical truth is based on what God wants us to believe for His own purposes. Biblical truth and human truth might not always coincide. A quick example is found in 1 John and says, *"Dear children, this is the last hour; and as you have heard that the antichrist is coming, even now many antichrists have come. This is how we know it is the last hour."*[41]

The verse tells us clearly that Apostle John, and indeed all of Jesus's disciples, went to their graves believing that the world was about to end. They expected the second coming to happen in their lifetime, but we know it didn't. Two thousand years has gone by, and we still preach this biblical truth, even though we all know if that had been a prophecy, we would have completely discounted it by now.

Why should the biblical truth be different from the truth according to our own human experience and knowledge? No one knows the exact answer, but Ecclesiastes gives us a clue. It comes from the mouth of King Solomon who says, *"I have seen the task which God has given the sons of men with which to occupy themselves. He has made everything appropriate in its time. He has also set eternity in their heart, yet so that man will not find out the work which God has done from the beginning even to the end. I know that there is nothing better for them than to rejoice and to do good in one's lifetime."*[42]

One possible reason for biblical truth is to make sure "we rejoice and do good in one's lifetime." The issue now becomes "Has God planted certain ideas that, while biblically true, do not coincide with the human experience and knowledge for this sole reason that we do 'good' in this lifetime?"

Let us look at this from a different angle. What would have happened if God had told us from the outset that Jesus will not come back or give us an exact date of His return? What would have happened if God said Jesus is not the only way to the Father? Chances are, we would have lived

---

[40]   Ecclesiastes 3:11

[41]   1 John 2:18

[42]   Ecclesiastes 3:10-12 (NASB)

our lives here on earth completely under the influence of the spirit of the world, and those still alive on the date of His return would have been the only ones to repent and ask for forgiveness.

In reality, people do not really want to live forever, and to understand this, one has to look at the miserable state of the aged who are lucky enough to die of old age. I for one do not like to live on beyond this point. What has happened however is that God has planted eternity into our hearts for reasons never clearly explained.

What we do know is people are told that it is God's design that they have eternal life, which they will spend in one of two places: heaven or hell. All the descriptions of hell are so daunting that one would be a fool to want to go there. We, therefore, pine for eternity not because the lifestyle there as described is particularly attractive for a living soul that has lived this life. We want to go to heaven because hell is completely unpalatable. We want to escape going to hell, which is an entirely different proposition from that suggested by Pastor Warren.

The Bible also introduces the idea that part of what God reveals to us is designed so we will not know His "hidden secrets." The objective is to make us rejoice and do good in one's lifetime. That is one loaded scripture, if ever there was one. It is also a passage that is capable of another interpretation. To make matters worse, if one reads the whole of Ecclesiastes 3, it hints at the possibility that we are no better than animals and that when we die, that might be the end. The three things suggested here are:

- God planted eternity into our hearts.
- He did it so we will not inquire of the things He has done.
- That way, we will do good while we live here on earth (our lifetime).

Beyond this caution, it will be blasphemous for me to continue probing because, if King Solomon is right, I would be breaking out of God's intent to plant eternity into my heart; so I will not know His secrets. In His infinite wisdom, God has done a number of things to keep us in balance. He has also told us that everything in the Bible is His truth; therefore, we should not question it.

From the scripture, we also learn that there is such a thing as a lifetime, and we know we live at most to be one hundred years, if we are lucky. When we die, that is our sunset. Life is over for us.

Pastor Rick Warren explains the scripture by saying we are meant to live two separate lives—the life we have now and the life to come when we die (eternity). However, if God only planted that idea into our hearts, as the scripture above suggests, what does that really mean? The Pastor deals faithfully with the reality of eternity for mankind. He tells us that, after we shed our physical bodies at death, a new life begins, which is eternity. Elsewhere in this chapter, he admits that if there was no possibility of heaven and hell, people would live their lives differently.

I found the above possibilities very thought provoking. It led me to ask the question "Is it possible that God, in His infinite wisdom, deliberately inserted some ideas into our minds just to enforce discipline while we journey through this life?"

This question might be relevant here because there are areas of scripture that God has deliberately left vague. There are also other scriptures that appear to contradict each other or contradict what we think we know.

For example, what happens when we die? The Christian answer is we go to heaven. Then again, the scripture says, "We are asleep waiting for the return of Jesus." That means all our ancestors since Jesus Christ ascended to heaven are asleep waiting for His return. Given the 2,000 years that have gone by, that is death, or what everybody other than those who read the Bible recognizes as death. It means you are no more. You have stopped to exist.

Again, to His infinite wisdom, God does not tell us when Jesus will return, does He? Is that part of the secret? Note another truth here. By planting eternity in our hearts, everyone since Jesus ascended to heaven believes Jesus will return in their own lifetime, and it is 2,000 years already!

GOD'S OTHER LITTLE HIDDEN TRUTHS

The possibility that God has made us believe certain things about Him and eternity to enforce discipline while we are in life is provocative. I class the many scriptures that appear at first glance to be contradictory to be in this category. Among them is of course the idea of eternity itself—the belief that Jesus Christ will return, the existence of hell and the fire that burns forever and ever, and the fact that God's fire torments but does not kill. In real life, most fires burn you to ashes. I, however, like most Christians, take God's word as gospel, so I believe. I take all these unanswered questions into my stride and choose to live my life as if there is a God and that whatever He says is the truth.

In my quiet moments, I reflect on the possibility that some of these things might not even exist, but that God uses them to keep us on the straight and narrow while we live. For example, we can look at the scripture that says, "Keep watch for you know not when I shall return." It could easily be something that was planted to enforce discipline in us as well.

As I said before, reality is Jesus has been gone for almost 2,000 years now. Each generation that has lived since then has lived with the expectation that He will return during their own lifetime. As the Pastor says, one has to consider where we would be if Jesus had given us the actual date of His return. The church would never have taken root beyond the lives of the Apostles, and people would have discarded the Bible. Moreover, maybe a few months before Jesus's scheduled return, they would dust up their Bibles and start to behave themselves again. They would read the Bible again just to be on the safe side.

I am not saying here that I believe what I am saying, but simply cautioning the reader of the possibility, no matter how remote, that God might have made us believe certain things to keep us away from His hidden secrets. The quoted scriptures above seem to suggest it.

Similarly, if God had said that if you die a sinner, I will burn you to ashes the moment you arrived in heaven, and you will be no more, it is very possible quite a number of people would have considered that a viable option to total obedience. However, the idea that we will burn not to ashes but forever and ever gets our attention. Simply stated, if these ideas had not been proffered, this world would have been more chaotic than it is now.

Likewise, the idea that there is another life after this one is attractive to many people for obvious reasons. Frankly, if that idea did not exist, it would make it that much more difficult for mankind to live other than according to the flesh.

Very few people would consider a place where you wear white and sing praise songs day and night an attractive place to live for eternity, especially given the way God has allowed us to live lavish lives here on earth. Who would buy a plane ticket to go to visit this place if it existed here on earth? We have grown accustomed to a variety of things that entertain us and keep us busy. Why, therefore, would anyone coming out of this earthly environment find such a sanitized place as the images of heaven we have been given suggests attractive?

The Book of Revelation offers us even more gruesome images of this place. We find all these ugly and fearsome beasts that are capable of such unimaginable destruction of human life scary.

Why should that attract us?

One reason why heaven sounds so attractive to us is because of the available alternative. If you're not going to heaven, where then are you headed? One option is to take the view that death is the end. When you die, one descends into utter oblivion, and there is no memory. That is what we observe when someone passes on. Life has gone out of them. However, God gives us this idea about eternity, which no man has seen, heard, or imagined (1 Corinthians 2:9).

At the human level, we accept death as oblivion. We rehearse that all the time when we go to sleep. We are unaware of anything. If we never wake up, we would never know we are dead. When you're dead, you're dead—you're no more, you're finished, caput. When we slaughter cattle, chicken, fish, or any other living creature for food, we believe they are gone forever.

When it comes to the human species, however, the Bible teaches us otherwise. Because we were made in the likeness of God, we do not die, at least not completely. Our human bodies die, yes, but our spirit and our souls live on.

If not oblivion, then what? Well, hell is the answer. We, of course, find this option so utterly unpalatable that we would accept anything in its place.

We can also ask, if there is hell, why not have the fire in hell just burn sinners to ashes the moment they get there? Why is it necessary to burn these people for ever and ever? The truth is we do not know why. As Christians, we are taught that God's Word is truth and that He never lies. Then is it possible God has inserted certain ideas in our psych just to ensure obedience by those who fear Him?

Now don't get me wrong. I am a Christian, and like you, I live my life believing that there is a God and that the Bible is His truth. If and when I die, I find there is no such thing as God, heaven, or hell, I have nothing to lose because I will be dead anyway.

I would be lying if I told a young person growing up that, in my own life, I did not enjoy some of the things that they enjoy doing, even though some of them may lead to sin. For example, growing up, I enjoyed going out and having a drink or two (can lead to drunkenness). I enjoyed going out to nightclubs and dancing the night away (can lead to reveling). At college, I enjoyed everything including dating different women (can lead to sexual immorality and sex before marriage, which is fornication). My idea of paradise, therefore, is that if I had a choice in the matter, I would obviously include all the things I enjoy doing in this life.

Young Christians today are learning to do many things they enjoy but in obedience to God. They have found a way of bringing song and dance into the church so they can partake in the things they enjoy in this life into God's house. In Africa, they have Christian concerts called Joyous Celebrations. We know the man after God's own heart, King David, did just that. When you come to our church, and you see me singing and dancing and making other joyful noises, don't judge.

Yet it is true to point out the staid atmosphere of some established churches do beg the question "What do you have against King David?" One hopes that it will not be long before the young find other Godly ways of doing most of the other things they enjoy doing. We clearly need to do more to keep our young involved in the church.

At this point, it is interesting to note that Pastor Warren uses a scripture that is capable of other interpretations in this chapter to advance his theory about eternity. He quotes the Bible that says, *"No man has ever seen, heard or even imagined the wonderful things God has in store for those who love the Lord."*[43] Amen.

POINTS TO PONDER

Write down what comes into your mind when you think of heaven.
Have you ever wondered if it really exists?
Read 1 Corinthians 2:9.
Now what are you thinking?

---

[43] 1 Corinthians 2:9

Have you ever wondered what it is like in hell?
Do you think that is one of God's hidden secrets?

Scriptures: Ecclesiastes 3:10-12
                 1 Corinthians 2:9

CHAPTER 7

Seeing Life from God's View

(Warren's Day 5)

In this chapter, we will learn about our life metaphor. That is the way we see ourselves. We are told that the unspoken metaphor influences our lives, and we express it in many different ways including the way we dress, the cars we drive, and the like. This life metaphor we are told influences our view of life and how we live it. Those who see life as a race, for example, will value speed and are in a hurry most of the time. We are told life on earth is a test, a trust, and a temporary assignment.

The Pastor says in this chapter that the Bible offers three metaphors that teach us God's view of life. The three metaphors are (1) life is a test, (2) life is trust, and (3) life is a temporary assignment.

The one thing that sticks in one's mind after reading this chapter is the idea of "the unspoken life metaphor." According to the Pastor, it influences one's life. I cannot claim that I understood everything that was being said in this chapter, but if we assume that people in general strive for success, the general life metaphor for everyone would be for success in everything they do.

The American dream influences the thinking of most, if not all Americans, but it does not always translate into reality. People continue to work at mediocre jobs while dreaming of the good life somewhere in their future. In fact, the majority of mankind never quite reach their success threshold based on the so-called life metaphors.

The earthly pressures to make a living do tend to move our focus from a God-centered life to our dishonest earthly lives. It is difficult in today's world to find people in a profession where some form of deception is not involved. We hear of second-hand car salesmen and their tendency to lie to make a sale. Auto mechanics have also been known to fudge the bill by overstating the extent of the repairs they carry out on one's vehicle. Tax accountants are notorious for inventing ways to reduce the tax burden on their clients. These are examples of Christian life that has not been conformed to God's expectations because of the pressures we face in this world to make a living.

After reading this chapter in the Pastor's book, I can't help wondering what the life metaphor for these people might be. All want to get ahead, but they end up doing it at the expense of someone else.

There are some professions that by their nature tend to drive people away from God more than others. For example, auto mechanics and trial lawyers tend toward the dishonest end of the spectrum while doctors, nurses, teachers, and the clergy are at the other end in the public consciousness. Nuns probably would tend toward the more honest end of the honest crowd, while priests have seen their reputations as a group tarnished in the public consciousness.

As we examine professional practices of the different groups, we see sin all around some of the things we do. We use deception in advertising in many areas of our lives for example, and we could go from profession to profession and isolate the areas where we sin as part of our working lives. For example, medical doctors and nurses as a group tend to be honest in their dealings with their patients, but doctors are known to succumb to the pressures of this world in their billing and tax payment practices. Teachers, on the other hand, can be honest on both scores because they are generally on salary, and the opportunity to fudge on their tax returns is less than that faced by self-employed doctors. However, they also fudge in their tax returns.

On the plus side, teachers and nurses, in their dealings with children and patients, respectively tend to exhibit some of the fruit of the spirit such as love, compassion, and unconditional love toward the people they deal with. Tax accountants, on the other hand, help the client (good attribute) by figuring out how best to minimize a client's tax burden. To get there, they tend to fudge the numbers and the issues. They will understate income and overstate expenses for example, but because that is the way they look at their work, they barely recognize the sin involved. Is there any wonder that we learn in the Bible that those who claim they have not sinned make him to be a liar, and the Word of God is not in them?[44] The Bible also tells us that if we confess our sins, He is faithful and just to forgive us our sins and cleanse us from all unrighteousness.[45]

One hopes that these verses and what I have said about sin in all areas of our lives explain why under the new covenant, God wants us to confess our sins every day and ask for His forgiveness.[46]

Yet there can be no doubt that there is little fear of God in the way we conduct our daily lives, especially in the workplace. One can look at farmers who underpay their workers to make a profit, to governments who will go to war and risk many lives using deception to get the country to go along. It seems that we are dealing with temptation in all these situations. More often than not, we succumb to it. This is disobedience for which God may discipline us.

How do we define the life metaphors for all these people? A typical teacher's life metaphor might be defined in terms of successive promotions that lead to the top through dedicated hard work. A lawyer in private practice will no doubt have a different life metaphor whose hallmark might be advertising aggressively to get clients and then building a solid reputation by winning cases before the judge and jury at any cost, including deception.

My point here is that, unless we reduce these concepts to the common denominator grounded in life's realities, we are unlikely to reach a conclusion that has a practical impact on our personal walk with Jesus. When we go a step further and explain to people that there is no one who is without sin, we can see immediately why we need Jesus in our lives and why daily prayer is a must, especially that part where we confess and ask God to forgive our sins. The mechanic who cheats and robs his customers blind is clearly living a sinful life. That should be the focus of our biblical teaching. It should aim to expose to the Christian how on any given day

---

[44]   1John 1:10

[45]   1 John 1:9

[46]   Luke 11:1-4 (The Lord's Prayer)

they might be living sinful lives and what they need to do to turn their lives around. In all this, however, we should remember that God's free gift of grace has to be tapered by the verse that says, *"What shall we say, then? Shall we go on sinning so that grace may increase?"*[47] There you have it! Our church leaders keep telling us what is in the Bible, but some are failures when it comes to equipping us on how to deal with this sinful world we live in. The problem that emerges is that Christianity, unlike its Muslim twin, has tended to give people a false sense of security. It teaches for example that, as long as you are under God's grace, your sins are automatically forgiven when you ask God for forgiveness. That line of thinking appears to contradict the verse that answers the question can we continue to sin after we have accepted Jesus as our Lord and Savior. The verse tells us, *"By no means! We are those who have died to sin; how can we live in it any longer?"*[48]

Therefore, we ask, does God forgive continual sin?

When you think you have found the answer, you're almost immediately challenged to define continual sin. Is living with someone without the benefit of marriage continual sin? There are no clear cut answers to these questions. No wonder many young people today find no problem living together before marriage. They reason that, when they finally get married, they will make themselves right with God.

Are they right or wrong in thinking that way?

Christianity is resilient in most situations, and it can be flexible to the detriment of many young people. It says if you confess all your sins on your deathbed, God forgives. That might explain why Catholics read you your last rights before you die. God, knowing all these Christian dodges, weighs in with another scripture that says, "Be ready, because you know not when Jesus will return." In other words, if you think you can dodge hell by waiting until the very last minute to repent, you might not have that chance as one can die in an accident or simply passes away in his/her sleep.

The question remains: Can the cheating mechanic be saved?

We can also look at the lot of the trial lawyer and ask: Can a trial attorney reach excellence without one form of deception or another? It is, of course, doubtful because, in that profession, winning has a lot to do

---

[47]   Romans 6:1

[48]   Romans 6:2

with creating believable storylines for judge and jury so the client can get off the hook. It is all about getting your client off the hook.

One can conclude from the growth of Christianity that, while it succeeds in evangelizing unbelievers into believers, it has done little to turn believers into God-fearing people who shun sin, and I mean all sin. That will not happen as long as we propagate ideas such as if you are under the cross, God's forgiveness is like standing under a faucet (shower). The dirt (sin) is washed off you the moment it lands on you.

Whether the people who push this idea are right or wrong is not important. What is important is that the teaching stifles any spiritual growth in the Christian.

LIFE METAPHORS INFLUENCING LIFE

Pastor Warren advances the theory that our life metaphors influence our lives. Whether the theory is valid or not remains questionable. Nobody, but nobody, has a poverty life metaphor, yet the bulk of mankind ends up there.

Likewise, many people from developing nations dream of being in America, the UK, or Europe because they see an America that glorifies the American dream. If the Pastor's theory holds, the apparent opulence of American life should influence everybody's life metaphor and propel them forward, but our reality says otherwise.

Even within America itself, the success rate of people of color is much lower than that of their white counterparts. We know that other factors can interfere with the will of God in many areas of our lives. However, if we were to go by what Pastor Warren has to say, maybe that was God's will. After all, He knew you before you were born and predestined you for that mediocre job, that stressful marriage, etc.

Nobody really knows the answers to these questions. On the surface, blacks in America have a God-oriented lifestyle that is centered on the church. That, however, has rarely translated into the good life for most. Their life metaphor cannot be that different from their white counterparts. Part of the problem here is that social, environmental, and political factors interfere with the process.

One reason we suspect this to be so is the overwhelming success rate of blacks in America in the creative arts and in sports, where outcomes depend strictly on objective measures as opposed to subjective evaluations common in the workplace. If you are a basketball player for example, you are judged strictly on the basis of your performance. It's whether you can shoot that basketball better than the next guy that counts.

LIFE ON EARTH IS A TEST

Pastor Warren also says in this chapter that life on earth is a test, and there is ample biblical authority for saying that. A piece I read on the website Acts 17-11.com said this about tests: *"The Scriptures speak of three types of "trouble" for the believer: (1) Discipline, judgment, or rebuke from the Lord; (2) tests, trials, persecutions, suffering; and (3) temptations or attacks from Satan. So is this present trouble the hand of the Lord in direct rebuke, or the promised testing of our faith, or are we being "had" by Satan? We should know, so we can respond accordingly."*[49]

It said these tests can come from God or Satan. God does it when we disobey Him, but the devil does it because we are believers. Satan is the prince of this world, and when we become believers, we are the "bad boys" in his kingdom. He attacks us. When God does it, on the other hand, it fits the crime, and we ought to repent. When the devil does it, we ought to persevere.

Then again, are we tested all the time? The Pastor's statement appears too broad to be useful in dealing with such a complex subject. Yes, we face tests in this life, but there is no way we can know for sure whether it is God testing us or whether the devil has found a foothold into our lives. For example, a tragedy in the family tests everybody, not just the one person involved. An injured child is a problem for the entire family. So who in this family is being tested by God—the father, the mother, the sibling(s), the grandparents, or just the victim? What if the victim was born with birth defects?

I am not arguing that this is not possible, but I am saying I am not convinced that this is universally so. There are senseless accidents that happen without God's direction, even though in this respect, Christendom postulates that the devil cannot act against you without God's permission. If one is a nonbeliever and is therefore in darkness,

---

[49]   Acts 17-11.com/tests

does the devil still need God's permission to hurt such a person since they already belong to him (the devil)? What about the not-so-righteous believer who is so full of sin that their only hope for salvation is the grace of God?

I also have my doubts about the basic accuracy of the idea that life on earth is a test. Every now and then, God tests us, but it's not a daily thing as the Pastor seems to suggest. Life itself is not a test, but from time to time, we are tested.

The Biblical tests the Pastor uses as examples were isolated and far in between in the lives of the people involved. For example, Job was already an accomplished rich grown man when God allowed the devil to test him. It is not exactly clear to the mortal mind why God chose to do that to him. It remains unfathomable to a mortal man that one can lose all his children and not be left with a deep permanent scar. The Bible does not address that issue.

GETTING THE CORRECT MESSAGE FROM THE BIBLE

Talking about Job in the Bible, one is reminded that, when we read the Bible, it is important that we draw the correct message God wanted to communicate. Sometimes the way we present the story of Job in the Bible can mislead and confuse the issues involved. Why did God tell us about Job? Was it to show that God can dispossess you and then restore you for His glory? Clearly not, even though some people say exactly that.

Second, the story is told as though God by blessing Job with more riches and new children, also blessed him with a Godly amnesia to remove the permanent scar that must have resulted from his tragedy. Job was flesh and blood, so we can draw certain conclusions from his experience. He lost his whole family. He must have grieved for a long time. The Bible does not emphasize that aspect of it.

There are so many Christian concepts that are based on a single biblical incident that we accept as capable of universal application when God might have used it for a unique set of circumstances. Therefore, we should be careful that we are extracting from these stories the exact message God wanted to reveal to us.

In the story of Job, it could be that God wanted to reveal His special but mysterious relationship with the devil; for we know from what was revealed that (1) the devil was part of God's inner circle at that time, that (2) the devil's mission was to roam the world looking for someone to devour, and that (3) the devil can only attack a righteous man with God's permission.

What is not revealed is the reality that the devil does not need God's permission to attack a sinner, and since we are all sinners, we are open game for the devil and his agents. Christians conveniently come to the rescue with yet another idea. By confessing our sins every day (remember the Lord's Prayer), we deny the devil that foothold he needs to attack. If we confine ourselves just to the story of Job, we are left to reach the common conclusion among Christians that the devil cannot attack a believer without God's permission. We forget that not every believer is necessarily righteous. The devil might not need God's permission to attack a believer who is not righteous.

We also conveniently choose to forget that the devil might already have license to attack the sinner, so he does not need God's permission. Since we are told we are sinners, God's protection might not be that watertight.

GOD HAS ENTRUSTED HIS STUFF ON EARTH TO US

The Pastor quotes an appropriate scripture that says, *"The world and all that is in it belong to the Lord; the earth and all who live on it is his."*[50] This scripture, along with Genesis 1:28 that gave us dominion over God's other creations on earth, tells us clearly that what is here on earth, including ourselves, belong to God. However, within God's estate, he allows us to own what we own.

We could use an analogy here based on the English monarchy. In England, the Crown owns all the land. Within that definition of Crown ownership, it is defined to exclude the inferior ownership rights the Crown gives to landowners within that Crown estate. Sure, the title of the land given to Lords and other landowners may be inferior to the Crown's sovereign ownership, but it is full ownership with unfettered

---

[50] Psalm 24:1

rights to sell that land to others or pass it to the owners' children when they die. The two types of ownership subsist together and are not in conflict with each other.

That is the same sense we should use the concept of God having entrusted the earth and all that in it to us. We say everything on earth belongs to God in that sense, but He allows us to pass what we own to our children as an inheritance. It does not mean our own ownership of what we own is not complete. It simply means it is subject to God's ownership. He is the source of everything we own.

Pastor Warren has presented the issue as though our ownership is devoid of any real property rights to what we rightfully own. That view is clearly mistaken because it stems from his refusal to believe that life is finite. When you die, that is the end of your life for all intents and purposes. Eternity is a whole new ball game, and the "you" that survives the "you" who was here on earth is a heavenly "you" that has no use for property in the sense we use it here on earth. Jesus's message in this area was exactly that where you are going is a completely new experience altogether and you will not need the things you needed here on earth. It is a place that no one has seen or can imagine. That is what the Scriptures mean when they say, *"No eye has seen, no ear has heard, and no mind has imagined what God has prepared for those who love him."*[51]

The good thing to emerge from the Pastor's discourse in this chapter is an admission and a recognition that life is a trust and that it all started with Adam and Eve. The Pastor quotes Genesis 1:28 and uses a version of the Bible that clearly highlights what God must have had in mind when He gave us dominion over all His other creations. Pastor Warren calls it the second biblical metaphor of life.

Yes, God did say at creation to take dominion of all His other earthly creations, but as discussed above, do not let this trust issue fool you. Our ownership of property within that trust is complete. At death, what we own passes down to our heirs. Though long dead, John D. Rockefeller's children and great-great-grandchildren continue to own his assets and still enjoy what he left behind. This is biblical. The Bible also says, *"A good man leaves an inheritance to his children's children."*[52]

---

[51] 1 Corinthian 2:9 NLT

[52] Proverbs 13:22.

In an article I read recently, the author[53] opined that "in order to leave an inheritance, not just to our own children, but to our children's children requires work, discipline, investing, planning and saving up our money." This teaching aligns perfectly with the fact that, in life, we strive for excellence in our chosen occupations because, if one fails to do that, they are most likely going to end up struggling to make ends meet. The only prohibition in the Bible against wealth is that we should not allow it to become an idol (another god). This is the situation that obtains when one starts to worship their earthly goals ahead of the Almighty God.

The word *trust* as used here should be given a special meaning because God also wants us to leave an inheritance for our children. Trust here is tinged with the idea that while you, the individual cannot take it with you when you die, you can pass it to your children and your children's children. Therefore, our ownership of what we own while we live is complete and unfettered, and most of all, it stays with your seed.

The confusion Rick Warren introduces is based on his attempt to redefine life on earth as we understand it. We have learned from the Bible that we each have a lifetime.[54] Life on earth, as defined by God, is finite. Within that lifespan, we do own what we own. When one redefines life to transcend two life forms—the life we have here on earth and the life we are promised in heaven—there will be confusion since, by definition, the two lives are different. For starters, the glorified bodies we are promised are different from our earthly bodies. Second, the things we have used here on earth have no use up in heaven. The mansions we are promised in heaven carry no mortgage, so why carry one from here to there? However, be warned that we are told plainly in the Bible that this heaven that we are talking about is *"what no eye has seen, what no ear has heard, and what no human mind has conceived"—the things God has prepared for those who love him."*[55]

For humanity as a whole, the ideas discussed might have some validity. Humanity, as defined to have started with Adam, and will end someday. We have been told that we will be resurrected and that His Kingdom will be right here on earth. In that Kingdom, the Rockefellers, the Fords, and the Waltons (Walmart) will most likely give up their

---

53   Grace Centered in Grace Centered Online Christian Magazine

54   Ecclesiastes 3:11

55   1 Corinthians 2:9

wealth. Until then, you and your heirs own what you own. Well, that will be a new world indeed—no Ford and no Rockefeller billions. Whew!

Reality is that nobody in their right mind expects to take anything with them when they die. Death itself signifies the end to this life and all its trimmings. Thus, while we can accept the Pastor's statement that what we own has been entrusted to us by God in terms of our lives here on earth, our ownership is unfettered and complete while we live and is passed on to our children.

In this chapter, Pastor Rick Warren finally recognizes that part of God's purpose for having us here on earth is so we can manage "His stuff" for Him. That is my suggested Purpose #4, which comes directly from the founding scripture. It is among the purposes explicitly stated by God in Genesis 1:28. That raises the question about the validity of Pastor Warren's original five purposes for a "purpose driven life." If this scripture is the basis of our purpose on earth, how come the other purposes stated by God are not accorded the same importance?

If God spelled out His purposes for putting us on this earth in Genesis 1:28, why then weren't those purposes used as a basis for Pastor Rick Warren's book, *The Purpose Driven Life*?

I personally think that some religious leaders run the danger of complicating life for their followers by failing to recognize the distinctions that need to be made between our lives on earth and eternity. Life on earth is a complete experience in and of itself. When that life ends, we enter a new life in heaven (or hell, God forbid). The two lives are completely separate and distinct, and the only link being—and this is a big if—to live this life in a manner that will not disqualify us from eternity. Our discourse with respect to our lives here should, therefore, be limited to what we need to do on earth in order to have eternal life and to recognize that the transition from one life to the other is seamless, if at all, for the true believer. You do not need to do anything else other than live this life in obedience to God.

Christians should not forget that, while we accept the authority of the Bible, the Bible only deals with God's relationship to us. It does not tell us about God's relationship to His other creations on other planets. Yet the way we apply the scriptures, we give them a universal application that might not always be appropriate. This assumption that God has revealed His character and nature completely to us in the Bible is at the root of several misunderstandings of scripture.

POINTS TO PONDER

Examine your own feelings about life and death.

Do you ever stop to think that, when you die, that person you see in the mirror is gone forever (from dust to dust)?

Now think about heaven:

- Do you see that "you" in the mirror walking the pavements of heaven someday?
- When your earthly body (dust) was combined with God's breathe, the spirit, you became a living soul. Does it follow that, when the spirit is withdrawn from the body, your soul also dies?

Have you ever been tested?

By whom were you tested? Was it God or the devil?

How do you know?

Scriptures: Psalm 24:1

James 1:12

Exodus 20:20

CHAPTER 8

Life Is a Temporary Assignment

(Warren's Day 6)

This chapter is a continuation of the last chapter, where we were told that our sojourn on earth is a test, life is a trust, and life is a temporary assignment.

There is little about which to disagree with in this chapter. Clearly, for every Christian who believes that when they die they will go to heaven, this is a given. There are songs that immortalize this idea, and one of them is "This World Is Not My Home" by Jim Reeves.

However, there are a number of ideas put forward by Pastor Warren that cannot go unchallenged. The idea that we cannot have it all on earth and that we are not supposed to be completely happy here on earth do not sit well with many people. If we accept that life on earth and life in heaven are two very different experiences, there is no reason why we cannot live completely happy lives here and follow that up with eternity.

Life on earth is complete and full of variety and choice. Personal effort can dictate the quality of life we live here on earth. Given our biblical purpose on earth, the quality of life also determines how well we will be able to provide for our loved ones.

God only requires that, in whatever we do, we do it in obedience to Him. Constantly devaluing personal effort that is directed at providing adequately for our loved ones is a disservice to today's Christian. If you agree that God put us on this earth to procreate, multiply, and populate it, then adequately providing for one's family is a noble Christian ideal. The only limitation is that it does not become an idol.

Pastor Warren's approach to the idea of wealth on earth as something that takes us away from the goal of being Christlike does not ring true. Nothing could be further from the truth. People like the Pharaohs of Egypt were not disliked by God because they were wealthy rulers and lived in luxury, but purely for their unbelief and disobedience.

Likewise, the friends of God in the Old Testament were men of means. They had plenty of livestock and servants. The few cases where being a man of means was condemned were when the acquisition of wealth became an idol, a sin. In the Gospel of Matthew, Jesus asks a young ruler to sell all his possessions and give the money to the poor and follow him (Jesus).[56] The young ruler of course did not take the bait, but that in itself did not make him a sinner. He simply chose to stick to the life he was accustomed to. Selling all you have and following Jesus is not a requirement for going to heaven.

False prophets in our time have used the underlying idea in this scripture to support scams designed to get people to sign away their money and property to the church. These scams are based on distorting what Jesus actually meant in that scripture.

The problem is sometimes we read too much into stories of the Bible, and in this case, probably more than Jesus wanted to teach. The idea that the young ruler might have valued his wealth on earth more than everlasting life in heaven may not be exactly what Jesus wanted to teach. The real purpose was to show us how the rich are less likely to be God fearing or to put God first in everything they do because of their wealth. They have everything they want in life. They only come to the Throne when bad things happen to them. These are things like bad health, bad relationships and business endeavors, and other misfortunes that money can't buy.

They do not come to the Throne looking for breakthroughs as the poor do. They do not need God to get off the unemployment line; they are the employers. They do not need God to save their homes from foreclosure; they own their homes outright. They do not need God to

---

[56]   Matthew 19:16-26

achieve success in business; they are already successful. However, these are the very things the poor are looking for when they seek to connect with God. The rich go to church with a completely different mindset. They go there to thank Him for their good fortune and dutifully pay their 10 percent tithe and offering. They have made it.

The poor are always praying for a breakthrough of one kind or another. For this reason, they tend to be God fearing, if they know about Jesus Christ, that is. They are more likely to commit their lives into God's hands. In fact, it might be good advice for nonbelievers looking for a breakthrough to turn to Jesus. It is as good a reason to turn to God for help as any.

The rich may look at this Jesus thing with a different perspective than the poor, especially for those who got there without God in their lives. They can rationalize this by saying I got here without Jesus, so why change course now? If you are an Evangelical and are trying to recruit a man or woman taking home $12,000 per month in our day and age, and you tell them they will have to pay 10 percent of what they earn in tithes, your success rate is not going to be that great. However, if you pray for a poor person earning $500 per week, and their pay doubles, they are most likely to be undaunted by the 10 percent tithe. One got there without Jesus, while the other got there because Jesus intervened in their circumstances.

It is also easy to see how wealth can become an idol or stated differently, their wealth becomes more important to them than God. These people can also use their wealth to insulate themselves against many of the things that beset the poor, and that leads the poor to God.

When everything is said and done, there are things even money cannot insulate you against. Money cannot insulate you against a bad marriage, a disobedient child, sickness and death in the family. In a sense, sickness tends to be the great equalizer between the poor and the rich in terms of their dependence on God. Even the rich tend to turn to God when sickness hits.

Likewise, the Pastor says we should not focus on material wealth (temporary crowns). In the context of our lives here on earth, that advice is meaningless and downright wrong. Just having a home of your own brings both stability and security of mind, and in cases where the house is fully paid for, it becomes the basis for leaving an inheritance to one's heirs.

It does not really matter how one defines *inheritance*. What matters is the effort you exert during your life here on earth to acquire wealth. It is a worthwhile endeavor. That is what counts and helps a good man leave something for his children's children. There is nothing unchristian about amassing prosperity. All God wants is that the process of amassing wealth be done in truth and in obedience to Him.

God also wants us to use our wealth for the good of those in need. By need, one has to assume we are talking about people lacking basic material needs that God has promised everyone, such as food and shelter and clothing and maybe good health. If I were a billionaire, I would adopt a poor country (Zimbabwe) and put my charity money in a microbank to help small farmers and businesses grow and employ the unemployed. That is development that transforms. I would have these new entrepreneurs pay 5 percent back every year in interest that would increase the bank's capacity to lend. That is my idea of teaching a man to fish instead of giving him fish to eat every time he is hungry. If God ever blessed me with a ministry of my own, that is exactly what I would do.

The proposition that life on earth is a temporary assignment, while true, is at the same time debatable. We were never designed to live forever, even though some biblical figures seemed to live forever (900 years). We need to accept the reality that there is such a thing as a lifespan on this earth. We prepare for the hereafter by living Christlike lives here on earth. That is the whole truth which also coincides with reality.

When reading parts of Pastor Warren's, book I feel like saying to him "Pastor, when you die, you're dead. Your body is six feet under the ground (from dust to dust). Your soul, a product of dust and God's spirit, is equally dead, though there are different authorities on this one. The fact that God's spirit that was in you goes wondering back to God is the central issue in the mystery we call eternity and should not fool us into believing the same old "You will be resurrected without thinking." That the spirit that left your body at death has no memory should be another troubling issue. One might ask: How are you going to recognize your loved ones up in heaven? Only God knows the answers. He is also the only one who knows how many of these spirits of the dead are there in Hades or shall we call it Sheol. Notice how suddenly these absurd questions are getting us closer to religions that believe in reincarnation. I therefore better stop.

The Bible sometimes adds to our confusion too. It says, when Jesus comes back, He will establish His Kingdom right here on earth. Since we are sleeping from the day we die until we are resurrected, there doesn't seem to be time for us to actually go to heaven in the first place. Here goes another biblical truth. Will God destroy the skyscrapers and the highways and bridges to make room for His Kingdom here on earth, or will we just continue from where the old world left off? Who will live at the White House and all the other state houses throughout the world? How about Buckingham Palace? Stop already! OK, I will stop now, but will we actually go (up) to heaven?

If we do go to heaven, which part of us actually goes to heaven? We know it is not our earthly bodies. We know the spirit came from God, so it has to go back there. What about the soul? "We are not sure" is as good an answer as you will get this side of eternity. The spirit will be in our new glorified bodies, and maybe the same old soul and the memory will come back. Mystery, mystery, mystery!

The bottom line, however, is that God's Kingdom will be right here on earth but we continue to talk about 'going up to heaven'.

We are bothered by the possibility of hell because we love many things God has decreed to be sinful. We love to indulge in many things that are prohibited. We will do anything to get money with which to afford and enjoy the things the Bible tells us are not pleasing to God. Yet there are times when one feels as though His grace by which we are able to ask and receive forgiveness for our sins also in a sense fuels our continued sinful lives on this earth.

I dare say there are many who believe that, at some point before they die, they will give up fornication, adultery, lying, and a whole array of sins and turn to God and repent; and all will be forgiven. In the meantime, they believe they can have it all without regard to God. The correctness of this belief cannot be properly established. If one is aware of their sin but continue to sin anyway, this is willful sin about which the Apostle Paul says is tantamount to rejecting Jesus.

Alas, the Bible does not exactly teach that God will not forgive the type of individuals who turn around on their deathbed and repent. The tendency to believe and rely on these permissive elements of our religion leads many to live sinful lives until they reach their twilight years. The only dark cloud in their way of thinking is another biblical verse that says, *"Keep watch because you do not know the day or the hour."*[57] It means

---

[57]   Matthew 25:13

you may drop dead before you repent and receive forgiveness. You may die without warning. Therefore, avoid sin.

POINTS TO PONDER

What does death mean to you: the end of life or the beginning of eternity? You are a triune consisting of body, soul, and spirit. Which part of you goes to heaven?
"You can't take it with you." Should that change the way you view wealth?

Scriptures: Psalm 39:4-5
                1 Peter 1:17-23

CHAPTER 9

The Reason for Everything

(Warren's Day 7)

We will learn that everything on earth is for God's glory. The whole of creation reflects God's glory. We live for God's glory. His glory can best be seen in Jesus Christ. Jesus brought glory to God by doing everything His father asked Him to do. He did that by fulfilling His purpose on earth.

This chapter is about bringing glory to God in everything we do, and one can but affirm most of what Pastor Warren has to say. According to the scriptures, after God created the heavens and the earth, the oceans and the fish, the birds and all the vegetation, He posed to admire His creation. The Bible says, *"God saw all that he had made, and it was very good."*[58] He then decided to create man to live in it. In addition to wanting man to inhabit the earth, He also wanted man to multiply and subdue the earth.

Because of what happened to Adam and Eve soon after creation, our sin nature entered this world, and it became a challenge for any of us to please God. By that one act of disobedience by Adam and Eve, Lucifer,

---

[58]   Genesis 1:31

also known as Satan, the devil took control of this earth. He became the ruler of the earth we inhabit.

There can be no doubt that man was created for His glory. Pastor Rick Warren is correct, and he uses scripture to make his point. He says when everything in creation fulfills its purpose, it brings glory to God, which leads us to the Pastor's original question: What on earth am I here for?

My reaction to that question is that "outside the biblical truth as set out in Genesis 1:28, does anyone really know?"

The Pastor does list five things that he calls God's purposes for us to be here on earth. We should worship him; we should love other *believers*; we should become Christlike in the way we think, feel, and act; we should serve others with our God-given gifts; and finally, we bring glory to God by telling others about Him.

There is nothing to disagree with here other than point out that the biblical purposes I have identified are different from the ones Pastor Warren has listed above. In chapter 3, I said our quest for eternity begins when we are born again. I identified the things that we do when we are born again and begin our personal walk with Jesus. There is no set age when one is required to begin that walk with Jesus, and a full two thirds of the world's population have never joined this personal walk with Christ.

Christians constitute only 32 percent of the world, and though we are the biggest group, we are not the majority. Muslims constitute 23 percent of the world population, and Jews a mere 0.02 percent of the world populations. Christians, Muslims, and Jews together make the majority. Makes you think, doesn't it? The biblical children of Abraham make up these three religions.

We all come to Jesus at different points in our lives and for different reasons. Some come to Jesus early in their lives. In fact, some do so as soon as they are able to make a credible profession of faith. Other's come to Jesus long after they retire from active employment, while others turn to Jesus just before death arrives. Now one can ask at what age is one old enough to make a credible profession of faith? The answer is there is no agreement on this. I have always believed that age was twelve, but I have no credible foundation for this except that was the age Jesus discussed scripture with elders in the synagogue. Pastor Warren's book has glossed over the fact that people have lives, meaningful lives I may add, before they come to Christ. His book addresses the things we do as believers, and we only become believers after we are born again. That failure to make this clear from the outset created in me a gnawing feeling reading his book—a feeling that it was too abstract to be useful in the practical sense.

That means, turning to Christ only adds a new dimension to a life that started at birth. Our walk with Christ has a starting date later than our birth date. The Pastor's book deals primarily with this phase of our lives.

In terms of our relationship with our Creator, there is the life we live before finding Jesus, and the life we live after finding Him (born again). According to the Bible, all you need to do is study (read and meditate) your Bible and obey God's precepts as represented by the Ten Commandments and everything else that flows from them and you should have no difficulty entering the Kingdom of God.

Having clarified that situation, there are statements in this chapter that are worth examining further. He says at page 58 that Jesus fulfilled his purpose on earth. Jesus's purpose on earth is explicitly stated in the Bible. He came to save mankind by His death on the cross. There is clarity in what Jesus's purpose on earth was, and it is biblical. That again raises the question: If Jesus's purpose on earth was as stated in the scriptures, then why is our purpose on earth not just as biblical?

In the same chapter, the Pastor has a line that says the "birds bring glory to God by flying, chirping, nesting, and doing other bird-like activities that God intended." Again, the Pastor can see clearly that God's purpose for putting the birds on earth is found in creation; yet when it comes to the human species, there is no mention of the fact that we bring glory to God by having children (multiplying), raising them, taking care of the earth, and having dominion over all His other creations as part of God's purpose for putting us here.

Why would birds bring glory to God by nesting, but humans do not bring glory to God when they reproduce? There is a major disconnect right there, and that again raises questions as to the validity and legitimacy of the five purposes the Pastor has listed as giving glory to God. To be fair to the Pastor, he makes mention of these things in other parts of his book, but none is given as one of his five purposes why we are here.

The Pastor tells us to ask God to reveal what our purpose on earth is. God has done that already in His Word, and most of us know what that purpose is. We believe that, in picking our way through life, step-by-step God reveals this to us. We believe we are led by an invisible divine hand into our respective purposes. To figure out our true purpose on earth, we need to look to those things we, as humans, do in common irrespective of our religious beliefs. To figure out our purpose in our quest for eternity, we can look to the Pastor's book and other similar books for ideas.

The Bible is clear on this point that, once you are born again, the Holy Spirit lives inside you and will guide you along the way. It is a process that lasts a lifetime. It is about obedience. Obedience to God from the get-go is the key to living our lives according to His plan and His will for us. When we do that, He has promised to guide our every step.

This analysis will be incomplete if it ignores the role of the devil in our sinful lives. The Bible correctly warns that *"Our struggle is not against flesh and blood, but against the rulers, against the authorities, against the powers of this dark world and against the spiritual forces of evil in the heavenly realms."*[59] We are talking about the same Satan who did not shy away from trying to tempt God Himself. He knew Jesus was God in human form when He tried three times to tempt Him. He will not refrain from tempting most of us, ordinary mortals, into sinful ways. He is at war with every Christian day in and day out.

In today's life, there are many distractions for a child growing up. There are so many ways one can miss their true calling. For example, children who drop out of high school will most likely miss their calling because they have not reached the minimum threshold of knowledge necessary to make informed decisions about their future. As parents, we pray that the child will choose college after high school. We realize that those who do not could be missing their calling by forgoing all those career opportunities that open up after college.

High school and college happen to be the two primary building blocks that lead to meaningful employment and a decent wage. I am talking here about life in America (USA and Canada), where the education systems offer what amounts to universal education through high school. There are many countries today where children, though willing and able, are unable to attain a high school diploma. There can be no doubt that this limits their chances in life.

When a child fails to at least reach these basic thresholds in their education, they are taking a chance they will miss their true calling in

---

[59] Ephesians 6:12

life. Most parents are aware of this, even though they might not be able to convey this to the child at critical points in the child's life.

A third failing in life is failing to do our best in whatever area of work life leads us. This can cause one to miss their true calling as well. Some people get a good job but fail to do what it takes to get a promotion or simply to advance in the company. The net result is they fail to fully fulfill God's plan for them.

The basic idea in life is to do one's best with whatever God has given you. That's not to say there are no high-school dropouts on minimum wage who lead contented lives. Some live happier lives than some doctors at the other end of the earning spectrum who are living miserable lives. Some of these brilliant people have become victims of their own financial success, finding themselves paying out two or more child support payments and alimony to former spouses, some of whom might have come to them as your everyday gold diggers.

There are truly no guarantees as each one's ultimate happiness is a product of many factors including the spiritual warfare all Christians must face. It is worth repeating that the scriptures that teach us about the devil's role in our lives on earth cited above is a *fact*. One feels reading through *The Purpose Driven Life* that Pastor Rick Warren has tended to underestimate the role the forces of darkness play in wrecking people's lives, especially Christians.

We are also told that we give glory to God by serving others with our gifts. There is nothing to disagree with here other than to clarify that point. In chapter 3, I identified this as "taking care of God's people." In the context of the Christian church family, this is a well-accepted proposition. However, God gives people gifts/talents in and out of the church as well.

Michael Jackson is a good example of someone God gifted enormously. He was one person who had such an exceptional gift the world at large took notice. Did he use it to serve others? The answer depends on who you ask. We could of course point to the hours of pleasure and tranquility his music brought to mankind. That's why we bought so many of his records, silly! Be warned, however, that some in the Christian world brand pop music as satanic. Then be the judge. His charity work, however limited, can be seen as fulfilling that purpose, but not everybody will agree.

I hazard to guess that, within the context of the church family, the Pastor is correct that we bring glory to God by serving others with our gifts, but the point to make here is that there are others outside the church who do and have done the same. It is after all the same God who created the human race.

The last purpose listed is that we bring glory to God by telling others about Him. This is also something that is true within the church family. Most Christians view evangelism in this way. Let us remember throughout that, whether we are Christians or belong to any other religion or are atheists, we are all creations of the same God. We are His children. Therefore, God's purpose for mankind should be universal. That purpose should apply to all God's human creations, not just to believers. The purpose God had for us at creation is the one that should be used for this discussion.

WHAT WILL WE LIVE FOR?

Pastor Warren ends the chapter by asking us what will we live for— for ourselves or for God? This is another major point of departure for me when I read the Pastor's book. I have never had any doubt that people typically live for themselves. At some point in their lives, people (just one third) realize something is missing and seek God in their lives. That is the time they are born again.

The problem when properly defined is that, while people live their lives for themselves first, when they are born again, those lives should become God centered. In reality, therefore, we live our self-serving lives in obedience to God. To argue, otherwise, is to deny reality.

I care about myself, my wife, and my children. Listen to the *my, my, my* in that sentence. Likewise, my brother cares about his wife and children and so does my sister. These people come first in our lives, and it is the same for *my* neighbor as well. I am the point of reference.

It does not mean that I do not care for my brother and sister as well. It means only that I care for them but not in the same way I care for my own immediate family. It does not mean I do not put God first. I do, but one is comparing apples and oranges here. Our love for God is of a different kind from our love for my family. In fact, the *me* and the *my* in this sense includes my immediate family as well.

God gave me certain responsibilities (and obligations) with respect to my immediate household. Those responsibilities and obligations are different from those I have for members of my extended family. If you put your immediate family in the innermost circle and then draw another circle around it, this second circle might include your parents, especially if they are dependent on you and your unmarried brothers and sisters. You can draw yet another circle in which your married siblings and their families are included. Finally, we can draw an outer circle in which your friends and church family are included.

The table below shows these relationships.

Note that in the second circle, your parents and in-laws are included. Though not your blood relatives, they are your spouse's blood relatives. Note one anomaly though, and that is the fact servants are included in that very first circle if they are members of your household. I know that defies logic, but as God has told us *"His thoughts are not our thoughts and His ways are not our ways either."*[60] Who are we to argue the point? The verse 1 Timothy 5:8 appears to govern the people who go into that inner circle.

The *Me* Table

Inner Circle	Second Circle	Third Circle	Outer Circle
Husband Wife Children Household - Relatives - Servants	Father Mother Brother Sister In-laws	Brother's Family Sister's Family - Include Spouses	Friends Church Family

God only requires that, whatever we do, our lives should always be God centered. A view that sees a God-centered life as being in competition with our natural God-given lives and the family responsibilities they impose has to be considered suspect.

---

[60] Isaiah 55.8

God is very much a part of our lives even as we love our loved ones to pieces. Loving God involves loving those around us first. The scriptures teach us that *"if someone says, 'I love God,' and hates his brother, he is a liar; for the one who does not love his brother whom he has seen, cannot love God whom he has not seen. And this commandment we have from Him, that the one who loves God should love his brother also."*[61] When we do not involve God in our lives, it is simply a mark of our sinning nature.

Attempts by Christian writers and preachers to separate life as either serving self or serving God is to my mind a basic Christian disconnect. The individual is the foundation around which this discussion revolves. It is you who wakes up in the morning and feels "I'm hungry," and then hurries off to the kitchen to get something to eat. This is the *you* you serve. There is no doubt you're *numero uno*. The issue is whether *numero uno* has God in him or her.

In concrete terms, I do not see how you can serve God without serving yourself. The Bible says, *"Love your neighbor as yourself*[62].*"* There you have it. God said it, not I.

While I understand what the Pastor is trying to say, we look and trust that God is directing our every step. We take care of our needs first. The issue is whether we then lean on our own understanding or we acknowledge God by telling Him through prayer, supplication, and thanksgiving what our needs are and ask Him to intervene.

More accurately stated, therefore, even the process of seeking God is part of serving our selfish personal interests. If we did not have a personal selfish interest to serve Him, we probably would not seek God. Truthfully speaking, we do not normally seek God for the benefit of someone else, but ourselves first, unless of course we are interceding for that someone else. Then again, if you can intercede for someone else with God, that means you're already into Christ.

Jesus preached the gospel to all, from rulers to the lowest of slaves. His theme was never that we should give up our professions or occupations and follow Him, but that all should serve faithfully whatever their station in life. Pastor Warren acknowledges this belatedly in his book on pages 282--284. He says, "It does not mean you should quit your job to become a full-time evangelist. God wants you to share the Good

---

[61]   1 John 4:20-21

[62]   Matthew 22:39

News where you are. As a student, as a mother, as a pre-school teacher, salesman, or manager or whatever you do, you should continually look for people God places in your path with whom you can share the gospel." I say Amen and Amen to that!

The true Christian teaching should be that God should be the center of your life, and not that you should give up your occupation and follow Him. Jesus's disciples were among the select few that got that call. God made them different from the rest of us by giving them His special anointing.

We should be mindful of the fact that there are certain messages in the Bible that apply only to them, just as there are certain passages in the Bible that apply only to Jews of that time. Christian leaders need to distinguish audience-specific messages in the Bible by explaining exactly what they mean when they say "We should serve God." Otherwise, this becomes one more Christian cliché not capable of practical application.

When you're a Christian, you're supposed to serve God in everything you do simply by being obedient and by showing love to those around you and those you encounter. You serve God by your example. The scriptures say, *"Slaves, obey your earthly masters with respect and fear, and with sincerity of heart, just as you would obey Christ. Obey them not only to win their favor when their eye is on you, but as slaves of Christ, doing the will of God from your heart. Serve wholeheartedly, as if you were serving the Lord, not people, because you know that the Lord will reward each one for whatever good they do, whether they are slave or free."*[63]

Therefore, when is one not serving God? The simple and complete answer is when what you do, say, or think is not pleasing to God.

I go to church, not out of duty, but out of an inner need to harness this powerful force that is my Creator that controls everything I do. I find it most powerfully expressed when I fellowship and worship with others. I am by my Christian nature afraid of displeasing God just as I would be afraid of displeasing a doting father. I please him by obeying His precepts. It is that simple. When I fail Him, I turn around and confess my failing and ask Him for forgiveness.

God knows we are incapable of avoiding sin altogether, and He admits it in the Bible. He has also made provision for it by offering us

---

[63]   Ephesians 6:5-8

grace, His grace. When we acknowledge our disobedience, He is faithful and He forgives us.[64]

Second, there is always a self interest in everything we do no matter what it is. When I evangelize, it is because I want to see the church grow or because of a need inside me to turn people to Jesus Christ. I derive personal satisfaction from all this, and I want to please God because I believe I will be saved, should there be an afterlife.

The Bible does concede the point by saying the fear of God is the beginning of all wisdom.[65] My fear of God is also based on my fear of going to hell. If there was no hell, it is doubtful many of us would be in Christ. The simple reason for that is most of what we really enjoy doing in this life is not pleasing to God. Without that fear, it is very likely that many believers would go the other way.

I say this very literally because I am aware that the things that entertain me ordinarily are generally not pleasing to God. If there was no law(God's law), I do not believe most men would realize that lusting after a beautiful woman was sin. Because we fear God, we begin to weed this sin from our lives one day at a time until we have conquered it.

I remember starting out as a young man and working for a Big Eight accounting firm that had offices at 2 Broadway in Manhattan. Some spring and summer days when the sun was out, we would spend our lunch hours standing around street corners admiring God's female creatures. Some women, for some reason, like to show off their good assets by the way they dress or shall I say display them. We were clearly lusting after these young women, and it was like a sport for us. We would analyze each one of the more attractive ones and make lewd comments about them. The comments ran the whole gamut—too fat, too thin, those legs, small boobs, the walk, the face—you name it. It was open season on these innocent young ladies. Did we know we were sinning? Of course not!

I can also recall my college days both in the USA and in the UK when we went out drinking. In the UK, we had our own pub right there on campus, and it was not unusual for us to drink one too many or even reveling through the night. We did not know then that what we were doing was sinful. As human beings, a good number of us enjoy doing these things, and even though there is no victim, God considers this sinful behavior.

---

[64]   1 John 1:9

[65]   Proverbs 1:7

You can also take the example of a woman who wants to find a good man to marry. Because she wants to be a virgin when she marries, she finds that men just keep slipping through her fingers because she says no when it comes to sex before marriage. A good number of these God-fearing girls end up giving in because they are afraid to let yet another man slip through their fingers. This is all sinful behavior, but we do have a God who is merciful and forgives us of our mistakes when we repent.

We can call this the paradox of dating because we can see clearly how total obedience in our sinful world is akin to swimming against the current. If you're in doubt, just look around you. It takes a lot of self-control and discipline and effort to be Christlike in the world we live in, and this should be acknowledged. We cannot go out there and teach these human truths to our young. We are duty bound to teach that fornicating is a sin, but we all know ultimately all you can do is deliver the message, God's message, and allow the individual to exercise their God-given right of a free choice. God does not even allow us to judge.

Yet I would be remiss if I did not admit that, for those of us who have given ourselves to Christ in spirit and in truth, there is tremendous satisfaction that comes from doing God's work and resisting temptation.

Whether you are a pastor or a saint, when you pray for someone and the very next day they call to say God has answered your prayers, there is a lot of satisfaction that comes from that. It is satisfaction tinged with fear, admiration, and reverence for the Almighty God because you know it is not you who is doing the healing; but a mysterious power working through you. There is a self-consciousness that comes along too. That feeling that you house within your body a powerful force that can perform miracles. Unlike a doctor who heals and knows exactly what procedures and medications he used to heal you, a spiritual healing leaves the healer-pastor/saint completely confounded and humbled because he has no clue how it all happened.

POINTS TO PONDER

Are you aware that you are the temple of God, and that He resides in you? Knowing this, what activities have you stopped doing for fear of displeasing God?

- Sleeping around

- Nightclubbing (reveling)
- Gossiping
- False witnessing (telling lies)
- Stealing

As you ponder these questions, what changes do you need to make in your life in order to glorify God in everything you do? Note that marrying a God-fearing spouse can help in the sexual immorality area.

Scriptures: Proverbs 1:7
                  1 Corinthian 7:2
                  1 Corinthian 6:18-20

RICK WARREN'S

Purpose #1:

PLANNED FOR GOD'S PLEASURE

(DAY 8 TO DAY 14)

CHAPTER 10

Planned for God's Pleasure

(Warren's Day 8)

We are told in this chapter that we were planned for God's pleasure and that we are expected to bring enjoyment to God. We are further told that if we are that important to God, we are not justified when we think of ourselves as insignificant. God wired us to enjoy pleasure, and He wants us to enjoy life. Anything we do that brings pleasure to God is called worship, which goes beyond music. It is not for our benefit; it is our life.

We were created for God's pleasure. We are told and we all tend to agree with that basic tenet. A review of the Bible shows that only the King James Version of the Bible contains that interpretation of that verse. The New International Version says, *"You are worthy, our Lord and God, to receive glory and honor and power, for you created all things, and by your will they were created and have their being."*[66] This is a prime example how one can use the Bible to back up their own view of the faith.

This is a criticism Pastor Warren has received from many quarters. In this case, it would have been helpful if the Pastor took time to define for the reader what it really means that we were created for God's pleasure.

---

[66] Revelation 4:11

The way it comes out on first reading invokes images of those ancient rulers who built stadiums where gladiators fought each other to death for the ruler's pleasure.

That's clearly not what the scriptures have in mind when they speak of God's pleasure.

The real issue seems to work the other way round. God wants us to please Him in everything we do. The scripture gives us the idea of what it is we are talking about. It says, *"So we make it our goal to please him, whether we are at home in the body or away from it."*[67] The idea comes back to living one's life in obedience to God. We should aim not to displease Him in anything we do, and when we do that, we bring Him pleasure.

I believe that, when Pastor Rick Warren speaks of God's pleasure, it means the Inventor takes pleasure in His creation when it performs as intended. In fact, he confirms this on page 55 when he says, "Even the lowly ant brings glory to God when it fulfills the purpose for which it was created for." One should caution in passing that comparison between God's human creations with human inventions misses the mark because these latter inventions lack the spiritual element that is so critical to humankind. They do not think for themselves or make choices.

This brings us back to the question why God created mankind in the first place in the context of the Pastor's book. One of the reasons He created us was so we can be fruitful and multiply and fill the world. If we follow the Pastor's logic about the ant, one would be forced to conclude that those who never married and have children are in some way displeasing God by not fulfilling one of the purposes for which God made us.

That view, while worthy of further examination, might not be completely accurate. We do have an affirmative duty to procreate, but there is nothing that says we are committing a sin when we do not procreate or that we are not pleasing God when we fail to do so. In fact, Jesus Christ Himself never married and therefore never had children, though He was certainly at an age when He could if He had chosen to. Jesus explains why people who make these choices do so or are forced to when he talks about eunuchs in the service of God.[68]

---

[67]   2 Corinthians 5:9

[68]   Matthew 9:12

The above reasoning shows how scripture can easily be used to uphold one's own view of God and what He expects of us. In most of these situations, the true answer is we do not know; and chances are, we will never know this side of eternity.

We are told that we bring pleasure to God by worshipping Him and that anything we do that brings pleasure to God is an act of worship. That means when we conform our lives to a Christian lifestyle; we bring pleasure to our Creator. We are also reminded that God is not impressed by ritualistic acts of worship, but He is moved by passion and commitment. We see this quite a lot in our churches. The passion is unmistakable, but unfortunately, we have no way of knowing the commitment these people have to the Creator.

The message that worship is a lifestyle is reinforced by verses that tell us to worship Him continually and praise Him from sunrise to sunset.

Reality, however, quickly tells us that if worship is not what we witness on Sundays at church, then there must be two definitions to the word *worship*—a broad and a narrow definition—and both are probably correct. Worship, as in what we do on Sundays, is something we could never do continually or from sunrise to sunset. That is because we all have other things to do. We have to go to work or to school and partake in a variety of other activities that have nothing to do with worship.

That tells us that this broader definition of worship is not what we mean when we speak of worshipping God in our daily lives. We are actually referring to our view of worshipping God in the narrow sense of putting everything aside and worshipping Him, which is exactly what we do on Sundays and on many similar such occasions. One needs to separate the two meanings of worship. The broader definition of worship is not accurate if we do not define worship as doing everything in our lives to please the God Almighty.

In normal usage, worship means being in a certain zone spiritually where we sing, dance, pray, and honor God. In real life, we actually set aside a time and place to do this. This is not to say the Pastor's message is irrelevant. No, not at all. It actually forces us to readjust our thinking and focus on the real meaning of worshipping God continually. It is about the challenges of conforming ourselves to Jesus Christ in everything we do and making this a lifestyle. The Pastor refers elsewhere in his book (page 88) to "practice the presence of God." Maybe that is what this is really about.

The Pastor brings his message home when he likens worshipping God to what we feel like when we first fall in love. He talks about how he constantly thought of his future wife once he fell in love. He thought of her while eating breakfast, driving to school, attending class, waiting in line at the market, and pumping gas—he could not stop thinking about her. This is a feeling all of us must have experienced, especially in those early days of falling in love.

At the beginning of my own religious journey, I could not imagine falling in love with Jesus, yet looking back now, I know the reason why. I thought then that I did not need him. I did not need him because I had other gods in my life. I trusted other gods more than Jesus. With my other gods, it was on an as-needed basis. I was free to live my life how I wanted to, and when a problem hit, I would go to the diviner for help. That is what people do when they visit diviners, fortune tellers, witch doctors, voodoo priests, and the like to consult about the challenges in their lives.

In my worldly days, when I needed to know, I called my diviner (otherwise known as a witchdoctor). When I had a problem, I called. When I was in doubt, I called. It was not exactly a lifestyle, but one went to these people on as-needed basis. In my culture and in my time, Christians saw no conflict between having all these other gods and still going to church and claiming to be a follower of Jesus Christ. That our living God is a jealous God who has little tolerance for these practices[69] was never considered.

The difference was I lived my life the way I chose to live it. If a woman other than my wife caught my eye, the chase was on. The fact that such habits were sinful to Christians never crossed my mind. I come from a culture where men still marry more than one wife. In such a culture, issues of fornication and adultery are not as clearly defined as they are in the Western world. My only fear when chasing other women was that my wife might find out.

Yet when I realized that I needed God in my life, things changed. Sin, especially that which I could control, quickly disappeared from my life. No fornication, no adultery, no reveling, and so on. However, there are certain sins one seems to struggle with all the time such as lying (excuses), anger (unless you live alone), and unforgiveness. These are hard

---

[69] Deuteronomy 4:24

to conquer. One is constantly asking God to help them overcome sin in these areas of our lives. We are aware of course of our tendency to sin and the need to resist.

Then there is another category of sin that is engineered by the devil himself. The scriptures teach us that *"our struggle is not against flesh and blood, but against the rulers, against the authorities, against the powers of this dark world and against the spiritual forces of evil in the heavenly realms."*[70] We generally refer to these powers as powers of darkness that reside in the heavenly realms. We know these forces as satanic.

As one grows in Christ, one learns how the devil can enter your life and completely mess it up. Christians like to teach that the devil attacks believers by attacking their marriages. The devil can enter your life through a loved one and play havoc with your life and happiness. The devil can bring you face to face with your own spouse's adultery—something that is sure to introduce strife in the relationship. Thus, though you can overcome your own adultery, it does not mean your spouse is like minded if he/she is an adulterer as well. Satan is adept at fighting marriages by creating these types of divisions between two people who once loved each other to death.

In churches, we see how this phenomenon can destroy marriages. Invariably, the spouse creating the problem never relates the strife in the marriage to their own ungodly behavior. People in these dysfunctional relationships do not always recognize the connection between their own behavior and the strife in their relationships. It is that strife that then fuels their unhappiness.

Instead of resorting to behavior that bears the fruit of the spirit[71] such as love, joy, peace, forbearance, kindness, goodness, faithfulness, gentleness, and self-control, they generally do the opposite. Because of their lack of understanding, these people become even more intransigent in dealing with their loved ones.

In some cases I have heard about, the devil can turn a loved one into a monster in the eyes of the spouse, to the point of making them see an actual unattractive evil person each time they look at their spouse. This normally happens when the two of you fight, argue, and disagree. This

---

[70]   Ephesians 6:12
[71]   Galatians 5:22-23

is a devil-inspired phenomenon that husbands and wives can resist by pausing and talking about the point at issue and even praying together.

The devil gets ahead of us by causing husbands and wives to blame each other over trivia because they fail to see the works of the devil in their strife. Instead of praying together to overcome evil, they actually drift apart in prayer because deep down they now want the other out of their lives. Eventually, instead of sleeping together, something that tends to heal and bring the two together, they drift apart and go elsewhere for sex—something that simply exacerbates the problem. They see that as the solution to ending the strife in the marriage instead of going back to basics.

The realization that some of these attacks can be repelled through prayer is what should keep God a constant presence in these troubled relationships. It gets so bad sometimes that usually one spouse comes to church, seeking a godly solution; while the other stays at home, pursuing the very ungodly behavior that is destroying the relationship.

The way Satan works in these situations is by convincing one party to the relationship that they are right. One is left wondering in these situations how a cheating spouse is able to convince themselves that they are not the cause of the strife at home. It is one of those mysteries of life only the devil can accomplish.

Other people have problems in the workplace. In some cultures, people go to witchdoctors for spells to jinx a coworker so they can get the other's job. However, when these people discover Jesus, they quickly learn that they can render these attacks ineffective against them through prayer. As they grow in Jesus, they begin to trust that they can overcome evil through God. He becomes a constant presence in their lives.

We all fall in love with Jesus for different reasons, but once in love, He is difficult to give up. Because to give Him up is to let the devil back into your life. The Bible tells us that *"the thief comes only to steal, kill and destroy."*[72] In his book, the Pastor seems to play down the dominant role Satan plays in our Christian lives.

---

[72] John 10:10

POINTS TO PONDER

Do you surrender your day to the Lord each day?
By praying first thing in the morning:
- you acknowledge Him;
- you give him glory; and
- you surrender the day to Him.

Do you quarrel with loved ones first thing in the morning?
Are you angry and short tempered?
Are you impatient with those around you?
- Getting children to school on time

Scriptures: 2 Corinthians 5:9
                Galatians 5:22-23
                Deuteronomy 4:24

CHAPTER 11

What Makes God Smile

(Warren's Day 9)

We will learn in this chapter that we make God smile when we love Him, when we trust Him completely, when we obey Him wholeheartedly, when we praise and thank Him continually, and when we use our abilities.

This chapter is about pleasing God. Clearly, anyone who is able to live their life in obedience to God brings a smile to God's face, figuratively speaking, that is. God is spirit and, therefore, does not have a face as we do, but the message is clear.

Noah knew how to please God and bring a smile to God's face. He loved and trusted God. He was obedient. He praised and thanked God continually, and he used his abilities to please his Creator.

In our own way as Christians, we believe we do these things too. The problem is we either do not do these things enough, or we do not know exactly what it means to love God and trust Him. There is an inherent conflict in using our abilities and trusting God. Typically, when using our abilities, we are relying on ourselves, but we know it is God who has given us that gift. This comes out clearly with athletes.

The question is do you use your abilities until you reach your limit and then turn to God once you reach your limit, or do you do both concurrently? How do we know when we are loving God? Doctors know how to treat most illnesses, so they prescribe the treatment, and all goes well. However, what happens when the patient does not respond to the treatment? I believe it is at these times when most of us start to look to a higher authority to take over.

The issue of loving God can be very confusing because we are told from the outset that *"if you love me, keep my commands."*[73] This reduces to one word—obey!

How do we factor in the need to obey and God's acknowledgement that, because we human beings have a sinful nature, we are sinners? He even sacrificed His only begotten son so we can be saved because of our sinful nature. If we accept the proposition that we cannot live perfect lives in the eyes of God, can we still claim to love God even as we continue to sin, believing as we do that, by accepting Jesus our sins past, present, and future are forgiven. God, in His infinite wisdom, does not give us clear answers.

We take heart from learning that there was always something flawed about some of the people God befriended. We learned that Noah was the guy with a capacity to drink one too many, to the point of forgetting himself. This is a useful truth to learn about one of God's friends. Abraham did lie about his wife Sarah, and Jacob, his grandson, was deceitful. King David was probably the most flawed of God's servants, and the list goes on. It gives all of us hope that, when it is all said and done, we all can be saved. However, can we claim to love God when we are disobedient?

Given the truth that we are all sinners and that people like Noah, Abraham, and David were no exception, the death and resurrection of Christ Jesus becomes that much more important to us. It means that our hope for salvation now lies in the redemptive power of the blood of Jesus, as opposed to our own personal effort.

We learn from the Pastor that Noah obeyed God completely. He loved God more than he loved anything else. He trusted God completely. He praised and thanked God continually and that he used his abilities to glorify God. All this tells us very little because we are not told how we come to this conclusion in concrete terms we can emulate.

---

[73]   John 14:15

There is an additional aspect about God's biblical friends that needs to be taken into account, and that is the fact that God actually talked to them. There was a basis for their faith that was real to them. They could seek God, and He would answer. In our world, God no longer speaks to us the same way He spoke to His friends in Abraham's time. If one heard a voice telling them to go sacrifice their own child at an altar today, they would run straight to the shrink, believing they have entered the early stages of insanity. We are not as privileged on this score as people in Noah's time were.

This direct interface with God has no parallel in today's world.

We know for instance that God spoke directly to Noah once he completed the mission God set before him. God said to him, *"Be fruitful and multiply and increase in number and fill the earth. Everything that lives and moves will be food for you. Just as I gave you the green plants, I now give you everything."*[74]

Just as the Pastor did not use Genesis 1:28 to arrive at his purposes why we are here on earth, he likewise did not use the above passage to the same end. Instead, he had this to say about the passage at page 76 (latest edition) of his inspirational book. "God said 'It's time to get on with your life. Do the things I designed humans to do. Make love to your spouse. Have babies. Raise families. Plant crops and eat meals. Be humans! This is what I made you to be.'"

"Bravo, Pastor Warren," I said when I read this.

It however reinforced the feeling in me that the Pastor had something completely different in mind when he wrote his book than what I was getting from reading it. Why didn't he make this exact statement at the beginning of his highly successful manuscript, something that clearly needs to be explained?

Why not align God's purposes for our being here with the very things God intended for us according to the scriptures. Remember, the Bible applies to all human beings. Some have chosen to follow it, and others have not. At creation, we were all created with the same purpose in mind. Why, therefore, weren't these very words of God's purpose for us used as the basis for Pastor Rick Warren's book?

Recall that, in Genesis 1:28, God said pretty much the same things to Adam and Eve, except for the fact that they were to eat only the

---

[74] Genesis 9:1, 3

green plants. God added meat to the human diet with Noah. To Pastor Warren's credit, he ends this chapter with a sentence that dovetails perfectly with my basic thrust that life is to be lived fully but in obedience to God. He asks, "Will you make pleasing God the goal of your life?" I say Amen to that too!

POINTS TO PONDER

Do you believe that you love God with all your heart?
If yes, how do you know?

Scriptures: Matthew 15:8
              1 John 3:17
              1 John 1:10

CHAPTER 12

The Heart of Worship

(Warren's Day 10)

In this chapter, the Pastor teaches that the heart of worship is surrender. He quotes Apostle Paul in Romans 12:1 where he says, "Therefore, I urge you, brothers, in view of God's mercy, to offer your bodies as a living sacrifice to God, dedicated to his service and pleasing to Him. This is the true worship you should offer." He tells us to trust in God and to admit to our limitations. He defines for us what it really means to completely surrender.

On the surface, one cannot disagree with Pastor Warren on the subject of surrendering to God. We need to trust in Him and put Him in the driver's seat of our lives. The Bible says, *"Trust in the LORD with all your heart and lean not on your own understanding; in all your ways submit to him, and he will make your paths straight."*[75] I love this verse, but like in all things related to God, you are never a hundred percent sure how to apply the verse in real life.

---

[75] Proverbs 3:5-6

The verse has its twin in the New Testament, where Christ Jesus Himself tells us to *"seek . . . first his kingdom and his righteousness, and all these things will be given to you as well."*[76]

Chapter 1 pointed out a good example of the dilemma one faces in this situation. On the one hand, we are told not to lean on our own understanding. On the other, we are advised to use all our God-given gifts to the maximum. In the "Parable of the Talents," the underlying message is that we should make the most of the gifts God has given us. Those gifts include our basic intellect.

However, where do we draw the line between making the best use of the intellect God has given us and leaning on our own understanding?

Every Christian is left to figure this out for himself or herself. Notice in this instance that you can be at fault for not using your own initiative based on the gifts and intellect that God has given you. You can be equally at fault for over relying on yourself. These concepts are not specifically defined. When in doubt, one can always pray about it. That's the advice one normally gets. That is one reason why some of us pray when we wake up and commit our day into the hands of the Almighty God. You are hoping and believing that God will guide your every step throughout the day.

However, the truth seems to be that this scripture guides us to avoid the two extremes of relying on oneself to the exclusion of God on the one hand and of just sitting there and doing nothing in the hope that God will provide all your needs. God indeed provides all the basics—food, water, shelter, clothing, and the air we breathe. In biblical times, it was rare for people to be homeless, so shelter used to be readily available.

In today's world, shelter is not always freely available. However, it is true that, while God still provides, He will not provide you with that dream house or that luxury car you crave for. He has gifted you with the talent and intellect to go get these things for yourself.

The problem throughout the Pastor's book is not so much that one disagrees with the ideas expressed therein. In fact, it is hard to disagree with the author's insightful look at Christianity. What is missing are clearer definitions of biblical terms and concepts so that they can be applied directly to the real-life experiences we all encounter in our Christian journey.

---

[76]   Matthew 6:33

Pastor Warren does a very good job of explaining what surrender means or does not mean. I would like to add the following comments to make this abundantly clear because, on first reading, I too missed his message. If you are a teacher, surrendering to God does not mean giving up being a teacher and devoting yourself to spreading the Gospel. It actually means the exact opposite. Continue teaching and be the best you can be, but do it in obedience to God. Use your situation to tell others about the Good News.

The Bible passage that best illustrates this says, *"You are the salt of the earth. But if the salt loses its saltiness, how can it be made salty again? It is no longer good for anything, except to be thrown out and trampled underfoot. You are the light of the world. A town built on a hill cannot be hidden. Neither do people light a lamp and put it under a bowl. Instead they put it on its stand, and it gives light to everyone in the house. In the same way, let your light shine before others, that they may see your good deeds and glorify your Father in heaven."*[77]*.*

We can also take a leaf from Apostle Paul's own ministry. He was a tentmaker and says with pride, *"You yourselves know that these hands of mine have supplied my own needs and the needs of my companions. In everything I did, I showed you that by this kind of hard work we must help the weak, remembering the words the Lord Jesus himself said: 'It is more blessed to give than to receive.'"*[78] He did not give up his occupation even as he devoted himself to preaching the Word. He supported himself by working at something to make a living.

When we speak of total surrender, we are not talking about giving up your life (as in flesh and blood). That part of your life continues uninterrupted. If you're a husband and a father, you still have to discharge those responsibilities to your wife and children in addition to surrendering your spiritual life to God. The keyword is to obey all God's precepts in everything you do. Your role as a husband and father, brother and friend, uncle, grandfather, nephew, and cousin should reflect the qualities and attributes that please God.

The Bible is replete with instructions on how one should conduct themselves in all walks of life. Instead of leaning on our own understanding, we should ask God for guidance. By asking God we

---

[77] Matthew 5:13-16
[78] Acts 20:34-35

mean praying, reading, and meditating on the Bible. The answers to your questions come directly from the Bible, and anyone who believes they will actually hear God's voice in answer to their questions are deluding themselves.

With the advent of the computer and the Internet, getting answers to our questions from the Bible has become easier. Google your question and the Bible answers by giving you a list of verses from which you will receive God's answer. Religious leaders need to make it clear that hearing God's voice is reading the Bible and accepting its authority over your life.

In marriage, the best way to approach this would be for the newlyweds to agree to accept the authority of the Bible going forward. They would agree that this is the way they are going to live as husband and wife; that they will be guided in everything they do by the word of God. My idea would be to enter into an agreement just like we do today with the prenuptial agreement, except this time we would agree to accept the authority of the Bible over our lives. Get that agreement signed even before you tie the knot, and then use it to keep each other in check throughout the marriage. Marriage counselors would use that as the basis for counseling couples when things go wrong.

Talking about marriage, we hear all those bad jokes about mothers-in-law from comedians and the like. However, what if we had agreed in that prenuptial agreement that the Bible verse says, *"'Haven't you read,' he replied, 'that at the beginning the Creator made them male and female,' and said, 'For this reason a man will leave his father and mother and be united to his wife, and the two will become one flesh'? So they are no longer two, but one. Therefore what God has joined together, let man not separate."*[79] If we agree this shall rule our household going forward. I am sure this verse would limit the influence of in-laws in marriages.

For marriages where infidelity is the root cause of the strife, the answer the Bible verse might give is *"But because of the temptation to sexual immorality, each man should have his own wife and each woman her own husband."*[80] Another Bible verse caps it off by advising that we should *"let marriage be held in honor among all, and let the marriage bed be undefiled, for God will judge the sexually immoral and adulterous."*[81]

---

[79]   Matthew 19:4-6

[80]   1 Corinthian 7:2

[81]   Hebrews 13:4

Now here is the verse every man would die for and would love to see in that prenuptial agreement. It is the one that says, *"For the husband is the head of the wife even as Christ is the head of the church, his body, and is himself its Savior. Now as the church submits to Christ, so also wives should submit in everything to their husbands. This mystery is profound, and I am saying that it refers to Christ and the church."*[82] However, be forewarned, today's woman has a different interpretation of this verse than man generally assume, so get an agreement on what it should really mean for the two of you.

Finally, the Bible teaches that we should *"not deprive each other except perhaps by mutual consent and for a time, so that you may devote yourselves to prayer. Then come together again so that Satan will not tempt you because of your lack of self-control."*[83] Good luck!

The above verses might not significantly reduce the divorce rate, but they will help eliminate needless arguments about who is right and who is wrong in every dispute that threatens a marriage. In our day and age where we have access through the computer to every verse in the Bible about marriage and other issues that affect our daily lives, the task of managing life would be made that much simpler.

Many marriages can be saved if, in those early days of courtship, Christian couples understood what these words really mean and put them into practice. At a point in their relationship when they enjoy each other and sex is a given, just understanding how one depends on the other as part of a marriage agreement can save many arguments and hustles later on in marriages.

The beauty of this teaching is that we can apply it directly to life as we live it. If you are the spouse who was denied your conjugal rights last night, educate your better half about God's teaching on the subject. This teaching can be applied to other troubled areas of our lives. Ask God (His Word, I mean) and He (through His Word, the Bible) always answers your questions.

The question is do we heed His advice (voice)? Do we even hear it? When we do, do we immediately stop the infidelity or other weaknesses that are killing our relationships?

---

[82] Ephesians 5:23-24, 32

[83] 1 Corinthians 7:5

POINTS TO PONDER

As Christians, do you accept that the Bible has authority over you?

Do you think this should be in a prenuptial agreement and be bound by it?

If you are already married, is it worthwhile to introduce this into your marriage?

Do you think it's a good idea to ask a pastor, where possible, the same one who officiated at your wedding to bless the agreement?

Scripture: Matthew 19:4-6
1 Corinthian 7:2
Hebrews 13:4
Ephesians 5:23-24, 32

CHAPTER 13

Becoming Best Friends with God

(Warren's Day 11)

In this chapter, we are told about friendship with God. This was the ideal in the Garden of Eden, but after the fall, only a handful of people ever enjoyed this special relationship. We become friends with God through constant conversation and continual meditation.

I considered this chapter the first real lesson I learned in this book. There are things in this chapter that I thought I knew, only to realize I was literally clueless. After identifying Moses, Abraham, David, and Job as the friends of God, the book takes us into areas of worship that have proved to be very valuable in my Christian journey. It is about intimacy with God. It is about changing one's attitude.

Pastor Warren begins by saying the obvious. He says it is hard to understand how one can be friends with an omnipresent and invisible God. He says we get to be friends with God through constant conversation. It is not a result of going to church every Sunday but of involving Him in everything we do.

However, that is not the whole story, and it never is with God. If I go on my knees and say to the Almighty "Father in heaven, I do not have the money but I would like to get my house repaired and my kids to go to camp this summer, and camp starts in less than a month," is this an appropriate prayer? I am clearly involving God in everything I do. However, is it possible that, when we pray this type of prayer, we are praying amiss?

According to the Bible,[84] that is exactly what we are doing. Then again, everything we pray for has a personal interest dimension to it. If you are a pastor and you pray for a healing for a church member, a positive outcome edifies the church. It enhances the church's reputation as word gets around that there is healing in your ministry; more people will come to your church. In the end, it comes down to a question of the extent of the personal interest that enters into our prayers.

I learned that, by involving God in everything I do, I was practicing His presence in my life, and this is part of the relationship with God that is so essential. I can introduce this stuff into my daily life and practice it without much effort.

Pastor Warren quotes from *Practicing the Presence of God by Brother Lawrence*, and I picked up another nugget, which is to pray shorter conventional prayers throughout the day rather than to try praying long sessions of complex prayers. He also advises the use of breath prayers throughout the day. He says single phrases can be repeated to Jesus in one breath as part of praying all the time and practicing the presence of God in our lives. From the examples he gave, I chose "Father God, I'm depending on you for everything." for my daily prayer.

These are invaluable lessons for all Christians, especially those who have pondered the verse that says, "Pray without ceasing." We can see from these lessons how one can do this without much difficulty. He explains that praying without ceasing means conversing with God while shopping, driving, walking, or performing any other everyday tasks.

Mixed up with all this useful stuff are phrases that are difficult to comprehend for some. For example, I have difficulty knowing when I am honoring God and when I am trying to control Him. My prayers and the prayers of most people I know are influenced by a personal agenda of sorts. It could be asking for a healing for a sick child or asking for that gate of opportunity to open or for a blessing to manifest. How do I know when I am trying to control God as opposed to honoring Him? I need a mental visual aid to fully comprehend.

The scriptures teach us *"not to be anxious about anything but that in everything through prayer, supplication and thanksgiving we should make our*

---

[84] James 4:3

needs known to God so He can straighten our pathways."[85] Such Bible verses acknowledge that our prayers to the Almighty are "needs" based. Even at the best of times, we pray because we want that personal relationship with God. We are in a sense of saying "I am coming to you in prayer because I 'need' you."

These are things church leaders, if they know the answers, should give us examples or visual images that bring these ideas to life and, therefore, make them capable of practical application in our lives. I confess that I still do not know the difference between honoring God and trying to control Him. All I know is it is bad to try to control God.

The Pastor reminds us that God reveals Himself through His Word. People are often confused when it comes to the practical application of this idea. When we read His Word, He is instructing us on how to conduct ourselves. If you are a husband, the Bible tells you to love and honor your wife. It also tells wives to submit to their husbands. Believe it or not, there are husbands who believe this gives them license to control and dominate their wives.

In all these things, we need to know first what it means to love our wives or for our wives to submit to us as husbands. Submission is not limited to that nightly romp husbands and wives have in the privacy of their bedrooms, but a totality of the relationship we have as husbands and wives.

Ironically, people my parents' age knew and did not question the proposition that the husband was the head of the household. What has happened during the last fifty years that has changed the landscape? The answer has to be the fact that women have been entering the workforce in large numbers. They are no longer as financially dependent on husbands as before. However, attitudes have also changed.

The love-your-wife issue can be tricky for husbands though. A simple staring point is to ask the husband if the wife is happy. For example, the husband might answer that she is unhappy. However, what happens if she is unhappy for selfish reasons, as when she wants that new car, and the husband knows they cannot afford it?

Others may want the freedom to act as if they were still single women—free to entertain other men. Sometimes husbands can and do this as well. The marriage is viewed as a sort of prison from which they have to escape. Most church leaders have seen this particular syndrome.

---

[85] Philippians 4:6

Nonetheless, if one goes back in the scripture, it is easy to see that you're dealing with deviant marriage characteristics because when you say "I do," you are also agreeing to forsake "all others" as part of your Christian marriage commitment.

Responsible married people have to make pleasing their spouse their daily mission. If you're the husband, ask yourself if your wife is happy and vice versa if you're a wife. That usually gives you a clue whether you are truly loving. Where the unhappiness stems from areas of life where you have full control, the solution is to make the necessary adjustments and restore balance to your marriage, but it should not stop there. It also means caring. When we concern ourselves with the causes of a wife's unhappiness, even when we are not the cause of that unhappiness, that is truly part of loving them. Adhering to all these rules about marriage is an example of "hearing His Word." God is talking to us.

In other areas of our lives, we deal with similar challenges. For example, "Thou shalt not kill," is a commandment. We do not kill in obedience to His Word. "Thou shalt not bear false witness" is another commandment—maybe the hardest for us to keep. We tell white lies all the time. Nevertheless, the point here is he is talking to us through His Word, the Bible, and telling us not to lie, not to kill, not to fornicate, etc. The question is, do we hear and recognize His voice? If we do, do we obey it?

Finally, we are told that continual meditation is another way of establishing a friendship with God. I personally liked the idea that if you know how to worry about a problem, then you know how to meditate on His Word. Just switch your attention from your problems to Bible verses.

POINTS TO PONDER

Do you involve God in everything you do?
How do you do this? Is it by praying two, three times a day?
Have you thought of reciting the Lord's Prayer when you have nothing in particular to pray about?
When you feel tempted, have you thought of "Father in heaven, lead me not into temptation, but deliver me from evil, Amen!"
Do you meditate on the scripture regularly?

Scripture: Matthew 6:9-13

CHAPTER 14

Developing Your Friendship with God

(Warren's Day 12)

In this chapter, we are told that a friendship with God requires honesty, obedience, and a desire for this friendship more than anything else.

The important thing the Pastor did for me was highlighting the need for honesty with God. He knows everything and sees everything, so it is pointless to be less than honest with Him. The graphic came alive for me when the Pastor talked about the Biblical friends of God as being less than perfect, but that they were honest about their feelings even to the point of complaining and arguing with God. The Pastor says God even encouraged that.

Until I read this passage, I was always fearful of disagreeing in anyway with God. His will for me had a finality that was disarming. After I read this chapter, I immediately started a conversation with God about my general state of poverty.

> *"Father God, my house needs serious repairs and my car is now*
> *a constant drain on my finances. I am smart and able bodied. I*
> *am in good health. I have properties that should take care of me,*
> *but it is as if my life is tinged with a reverse Midas touch of sorts.*

Why God? Answer me! What have I done to You about which You're so unforgiving?"

I was aware of my sins of course, and doubly aware that, for some of them, any other man of the world—I mean flesh and blood—could never forgive me for the things I had done while living according to the flesh. I was not talking to any ordinary man of the flesh here though. I was talking to the Almighty God—the God who forgives.

Reading this chapter, I felt emboldened because it opened up this new channel of conversation with God. I had a grievance, and I was going to make my point with the Divine Father.

"Father God, the father of Jesus, the God who said let there be light and there was light, the Alpha and the Omega, why am I cursed? Why this curse of slow progress and fruitless hard work?"

As a lay preacher in my church, I wanted God to answer me so I could fix the problem. This forced me to look deeper into my past lifestyle. I was bringing up all sorts of things I had done that in my new Christian walk were the equivalent of capital crimes, but that were just part of my life when I lived by the flesh. My mind kept wondering which one was responsible for the curse I was sure I was living under.

At these times, people start wondering which past sins might be at work here. If they had an affair with someone's wife, that is a biggie. They begin to wonder if God was punishing them for that transgression. If they owed money to a friend that they could not pay back, they examine that situation with the same goals in mind. They are wondering if that is where the fault line with God is. If they were into the occult for the better part of their adult lives and trusted in those other gods, they wonder if they are being punished for that? They remember that, before being born again, they consulted with mediums and witchdoctors for answers to problems they can now get resolved through prayer.

There is nothing wrong with looking back, but this is also the time to remember that, when you accept Jesus as your Lord and Savior and confess all your sins, from that day on, your past, present, and future sins are forgiven. You are now under the cross, and all that is left to do is transform your life into a Christlike life by cultivating good spiritual habits.

In my case, I began to recall God's promises to me through His Word, the Bible. I remembered the verse that says, *"Therefore, if anyone is in Christ, he is a new creation; the old has gone, the new has come!"*[86] When you're born again, you truly qualify for His forgiveness of your past sins.

The anxiety about one's past transgressions does not end here because there are other panic doors that can be opened in one's mind. What if I am not being forgiven because I have not forgiven those who have trespassed against me? Even though one knows deep down that they have forgiven all those who trespassed against them, there is always room for doubt, and God makes it clear this is a biggie. Thus, even though they are not the type to harbor a grudge, the doubts flood in.

This is one of those areas in the Christian experience where one is never too sure whether they have truly been forgiven. There are people who have taken advantage of you to such an extent that the moment their name is mentioned, your whole body tenses up. Could this be a sign you have not quite forgiven that person? There is no way to know for sure.

Over the years, I have come across so many jilted lovers who find it difficult to forgive—so many abused wives who have difficulty forgiving. I always think about all those single mothers in my church who blame their exes for their present predicament. This is not difficult to understand. Men have this habit of leaving their wives and children for much younger women. Men forget that these mothers bear the scars of childbirth, and in some cases, their disfiguring effects for life. They look in the mirror and see a disfigured body all due to the now departed ex-husband who is now living with a woman younger than their oldest child, and you're asking them to forgive. Oh, hell no!

When you read a book, and it provokes you into such soul searching, you know the message has hit home; and that is the mark of a good book. I am emboldened to claim my deliverance from whatever bondage I was in after reading this book, and I am able to argue my point with my Creator.

> *"Father God, I am following all your precepts and where I fall short, I come to you in confession, so what are your reasons for not forgiving me, Lord. Give me my freedom Oh Lord, for I have renounced all ungodliness in my life and submitted wholly to you."*

---

[86] 2 Corinthians 5:17

Just then new doubts start to flood in again. You think maybe you're praying amiss, so you make the necessary adjustments to your prayer lines and continue praying.

> *"Father God, you are the God that can see my heart; therefore you know my desires and my needs; please Father God, take them and make the necessary adjustments to conform them to your will so what you will grant me will be in accordance with your will."*

Choosing to obey God in faith is something most Christians have been conditioned to do. We have faith that God will do what He says He will do. We trust that, despite our sins, His plans for us are for good and not evil and on that basis we pray and wait for answers.

I took to heart the Pastor's allusions to God cherishing the simple acts of obedience to prayers, praises, or offerings. He quotes the Bible which asks *"what pleases the Lord more: burnt offerings and sacrifices or obedience to his voice? It is better to obey than to sacrifice."*[87] This validates those simple acts of obedience we take for granted. They are important, and it makes sense. What is the point of an offering if one cannot do good to those around Him?

We also learn that, to be friends with God, we need to care about the things He cares about and that we should desire this friendship more than anything else. I stumbled on the idea that I should desire my friendship with God more than any other friendships. While our friendship with God looms large, our earthly friendships have a certain immediacy that our relationship with God does not. We talk, touch, hear, and see our earthly friends. Coming home to a loving spouse has a certain quality to it that is immediate and more intimate. His/Her absence from your life is immediately noticed, and the intimacy aspects of the relationship loom large. God's presence or absence, on the other hand, is of a completely different dimension and should not really be compared. The essential difference is that, together with my earthly friends, we can both enjoy our friendship with God.

The type of reasoning used by the Pastor here is misleading because you are not comparing like with like. For example, we all need air just to breathe in order to stay alive. Without air for as little as three or so

---

[87]   2 Samuel 15:22

minutes, we will be dead. We should desire air more than anything else in the world. That is true, but here on earth, air is a prerequisite for life. Without it, there is no life. In fact, if given a choice between God and air, everyone will choose air because, while they can live without God, they cannot live without air.

However, it would be wrong to conclude that air is more important than God. It should not take long for the average person to figure out that by comparing things that have no common basis for comparison I can make a very meaningless statement sound real. Even though people will choose air to breath ahead of God, that does not change the fact that God is the most important force in the universe. Nevertheless, choosing God over the air we breathe is choosing death over life. We, therefore, should be wary of meaningless statements that can stress our brains when they have no substance.

My view is that, while God's friendship is important, it transcends all these other friendships and finds expression in them and not the other way round. You cannot have a meaningful relationship with God if you have no meaningful friendships with your brothers and sisters here on earth.

I desire a friendship with God because I am convinced that, through it, I can reach all my other goals in life, including building friendships that really matter. It seems to me that there is always this personal agenda to our relationship with God. Whether one does it because it brings them the peace of mind they seek does not matter. The truth is there seems to be something in it for the individual who is praying.

King David must be the one person who had a long and continuous friendship with God. He must hold the crown for the sheer ability to pray and bare it all. We are talking about a guy who could get a mistress's husband killed and go two years before he realizes he had done something wrong. It took a man of God to tell him so. Yet once convicted, he had the humility to cry to God for forgiveness.

Throughout the Psalms, King David cried to God for protection, for a blessing, or simply to get God to deal with his enemies. His imprecatory prayers such as Psalm 109, which is considered by some theologians to be contrary to the teachings of Christ are examples of the extent to which he used God. The other imprecatory prayers are Psalms 5, 10, 17, 35, 58, 59, 69, 70, 79, 83, 137 and 140. The word *imprecate* means to pray evil against someone. The personal agenda in these and other Psalms is very clear.

As a relatively new Christian, I found myself wrestling with all these issues. I tried Psalm 109, but after verse 7, it got too heavy going for me. Hazy memories of what the Bible says about "vengeance is mine" start surfacing in my mind as I went through the process of trying to assimilate all the new insights I was getting from reading the Pastor's book. I did not want my enemy's children to become orphans[88] as the Psalm would seem to suggest.

Then there was King Hezekiah. He was another one whose prayer was for God to give him more time on this earth. His prayer was answered, and he got fifteen more years.[89] Again, we see the message that we are invited to pray to God for all our needs and wants. It is up to Him to decide whether we are praying amiss or not. It cannot be up to you because, as we have seen, we are invited to come to Him with all our problems. God decides whether to deny your prayer, grant it, or wait on it.

The discussion about developing a friendship with God is incomplete without factoring in the devil's counter efforts against you. After all, his specialty and that of his agents is to interfere with our relationship with God. This is particularly so given the fact that, at creation, God had devised this perfect relationship with Adam and Eve. It was the devil that disrupted that relationship, and this continues to the present day.

The devil does not particularly like us to have a perfect relationship with God. He does not want it to develop unhindered; therefore, he is constantly putting roadblocks in every believer's way. The roadblocks take many forms depending on the circumstances of the believer.

Satan can claim legal rights against you[90] on the basis of your sin and the covenants your ancestors entered into with the forces of darkness way back then. The thing to remember though is that the fact you are living under a curse on earth does not mean you will not go to heaven. God only judges you on the basis of your own sin. It means that you are going to live a troubled life here on earth—something God never planned for you.

In my Zimbabwe culture, for example, it is said families can offer a newly born baby to forces of darkness to settle old scores. Old scores

---

[88]   Psalm 109:8-9

[89]   Isaiah 38:5

[90]   Ephesians 4:25-27

are sins of our ancestors that have not been requited. That child, as he/ she grows, can develop issues that require serious deliverance prayers to overcome. Spirit husbands and spirit wives come into the innocent child's life in this way as well.

Satan's strongest entry point into our lives remains our marriages. Here, the devil is able to use one partner against the other to achieve his goals. He can introduce strife into the marriage that makes it difficult for one party to remain true to the Almighty. We all know that anger and strife interfere with our fellowship with God. The devil can use your spouse to provoke you to anger day in and day out.

Here is the catch. When stuck in a marriage that does not work, modern man and woman see divorce as the answer. However, the scriptures say God hates divorce, and the believer can go for years struggling to make the decision to divorce out of the fear of God. That leads to a situation that is never conducive to a healthy relationship with God, and the devil is the winner.

In many people's eyes, divorce is a sin. It might not be if the divorce is the consequence of a wife's fornication. Worse still, for those who divorce and remarry, their fate in the eyes of God remains murky. Does He ever forgive divorcees, especially those who have since remarried? What about those who remarried before coming to Christ? Different people will give you different answers because God did not clearly clarify the issue. In a world where half the preachers are divorcees, an honest answer is difficult to come by. I am guided, however, by the knowledge that God forgives all sins. Therefore, the best you can do is pray about it and ask for His forgiveness.

We also need to remember that, at the time this was written, men were allowed to marry many wives. King David and King Solomon both had multiple wives. The pressure was on protecting women from being cast out of a marriage. It seems as though there were no consequences for a man with many wives who divorced one of them. Thus, if women view this particular scripture with some degree of suspicion, we should not blame them. The situation became clearer under the new covenant. Jesus was against divorce except for a woman's adultery.

If you feel confused, you are not alone, welcome to my wonderful walk with Jesus. He will reveal all this to you, if not today it will come in God's time. Amen!

POINTS TO PONDER

Identify the elements that enter into your earthly relationships.
Identify the factors that interfere with these relationships.
Identify the factors that interfere with your relationship with God.
What action can you take to mitigate these factors?
How can one develop a friendship with God that transcends real-life friendships like the one between husband and wife?

Scriptures: Ephesians 4:25-27
                Psalm 109:1-7

CHAPTER 15

Worship That Pleases God

(Warren's Day 13)

In this chapter, we are told that worship pleases God when it is accurate, authentic, thoughtful, and practical. We worship in spirit in response to God's spirit, and the author distinguishes the spirit involved in worship from the soul.

This chapter I found heavy going.

First, we learn what worship isn't. However, at the end of it all, we learn that worship is exalting God in everything we do. The Apostle Paul says, *"Therefore, I urge you, brothers, in view of God's mercy, to offer your bodies as living sacrifices, holy and pleasing to God—this is your spiritual act of worship."*[91] That means we have to be fully engaged body and soul in worshipping God.

Worship must be based on the scriptures to be accurate.

That sounds simple enough, but I quickly got lost when the discussion moved to worshipping God in truth and in spirit. The truth part was no bother because it simply means we should worship God as revealed to us in the scriptures. If we invent our own image of God in our minds, we will not be worshipping in truth.

---

[91] Romans 12:1

The spirit part however created a certain degree of confusion in my mind. The Pastor was quick to warn that the spirit we are talking about is not the Holy Spirit, but the spirit within us, our own spirit, the one God put into our bodies to give "us" life.

Fair enough, but to be honest, until I read Rick Warren's book, I never made that distinction in my own mind. Now that the issue had been brought into sharp focus in my mind, I found myself struggling to grasp the Christian concept of spirit. I discuss this issue in more detail in chapter 22.

When Pastor Rick Warren speaks of worshipping that pleases God, worshipping in spirit and truth, he is talking about the soul because he quickly quotes Jesus as saying, *"Love God with all your heart and soul."*[92] Jesus is, of course, was not just talking about the heart that pumps blood to all areas of our bodies, he was also talking about the brain—that part of you that thinks.

The problem we find is the Bible uses the words *spirit* and *soul* interchangeably. There are verses that will say spirit when they really mean the soul. In the following scripture, it is said that Jesus called out in a loud voice, *"Father into your hands I commit my spirit."*[93] Here, we learn that spirit is that part of us that survives death. It is the spirit and not the soul. We have been told that the soul is the part of us that is involved in worship. Clearly, we need to know what really is the soul. From Genesis, we learn that God breathed in Adam's nostrils, and the combination of this breath and dust made us a living soul. In worship, it would seem the whole of me is involved. I use my body to dance to my God, and my spirit to relate to God, and my soul to relate to others around me, my fellow worshippers.

As one explores the subject of spirit and soul and their functions, it can become very overwhelming. When theological writers use the words spirit, heart, soul, mind or conscience, forgive them if they leave you confused. It is an area that lacks clarity.

That is why I choose to believe that the part of me that worships the Almighty is my soul, the product of my spirit and physical body, because all of me is involved in worship. There is singing, dancing, and playing of

---

[92]   Luke 10:27; Deuteronomy 6:5

[93]   Luke 23:46

instruments in worship that pleases God. The soul is just that part of me that gives me my personality, character, and identity.

My research on this topic also led me among other things to a blog by Adrian Warnock on this subject. What I liked about it was that he used scripture to reveal worship that pleases God. He said he summarized Dr. Sam Storms's "Worship that Pleases God" (Psalms 92-98) as:

1. Worship that pleases God is perpetual and constant. (Psalm 92:2)
2. Worship that pleases God is instrumental. (Psalm 150)
3. Clearly, God delights in joyful worship. (Psalm 92:4)
4. Worship that pleases God is grounded in the recognition and celebration of His greatness. (Psalm 92:5)
5. Worship that pleases God is both loud and logical . . . Note well that worship here (in the Psalms) entails noisy songs.
6. Worship that pleases God is physical. (Psalm 95:6)
7. Worship that pleases God is fresh and creative. (Psalm 33:3, Psalm 40:3, Psalm 96:1, Psalm 98:1, Psalm 144:9, Psalm 149:1)
8. Worship that pleases God is public. (Psalm 96:3)
9. Worship that pleases God ascribes glory to His name.
10. God is especially honored when the whole of creation joins in celebrating His goodness and greatness. (Psalm 96:11-13a).

The Pastor rounds out this chapter by telling us that worship should be thoughtful and that it should be practical. The Bible says, *"They worship me in vain; their teachings are but rules taught by men."*[94]

Rhoel Lomahan in a piece in the West Loop Church UBF tells us that this verse means God is not pleased with unconscious worship and by that we mean thoughtless singing of hymns, perfunctory praying of clichés, or careless exclamations of "Praise the Lord" because we can't think of anything else to say at that moment. Unless your mind is engaged, worship becomes a meaningless motion or empty emotion. This is the problem Jesus called "vain repetitions."

Finally, my research led me to Pastor David Cho Yonggi Cho and his view of praying in the spirit which is to pray in tongues. He prefers that type of prayer because one can go on for hours praying in the spirit. He also recommends what he calls the Tabernacle Prayer.

---

[94] Matthew 15:9

While God remains a mystery, there are many areas of the scripture that remain a mystery or a source of confusion to many Christians as well. The best advice one can give when in doubt is to have faith, which, by definition, is the substance of things hoped for and the evidence of things not seen.

POINTS TO PONDER

Examine your worship practices.
Do they please God according to the scriptures?
Are you a spectator at Sunday worship or an active participant?
If a spectator, is this due to your personal preference or church dogma?
Review the Psalms above for guidance on what really pleases God according to the scriptures.

Scriptures: Romans 12:1
     Matthew 15:9

CHAPTER 16

When God Seems Distant

(Warren's Day 14)

We are told that there are times when God feels distant, and those happen to be times when things are not going so well in our lives. We are told that worship is praising God despite the pain, thanking Him through a trial, and trusting Him when tempted. We should not be afraid to tell Him how we feel, and we should focus on His unchanging nature. We should always remember what God has already done for us.

We are reminded in this chapter of those times when God seems absent from our lives, and we wonder what is going on. The chapter also invokes the memory of Job and how God allowed him to lose everything.

A big issue that comes up in my mind every time Christian writers bring up the subject of God's friends is the failure to mention that things were different then. The God who accompanied the Jewish people out of Egypt into Canaan has since changed his mode of communication. Things were very different then. God actually talked to these people in His own voice. There was a conversation going on between God and His friends. That friendship was close to the real-life friendships we enjoy with our own real-life friends, except for the fact that it lacked a physical dimension.

It has been a while since God has spoken in the same way with any known human being. It would seem that since the Bible, as we know it was last written, God got out of the business of speaking directly with mankind the way he used to speak to Moses and the others.

I am aware that many pastors today claim that God has told them this and that, but our continued use of Old Testament stories about God speaking to ordinary human beings needs to be handled with care. They are good teaching aids, but relevance might be a real issue.

A relevant scripture to keep in mind is *"I have heard what the prophets say who prophesy lies in my name. They say, 'I had a dream! I had a dream!' How long will this continue in the hearts of these lying prophets, who prophesy the delusions of their own minds?"*[95] We should always keep these verses at the back of our minds every time we hear someone claim God told them something.

God does not talk to people in human terms anymore. He has not done so since the first century (AD 95-96) when the last canon of the New Testament, Revelation, was closed. It is unlikely He will do so anytime soon.

When God feels distant, we should not accuse Him for neglecting us. The truth is all our lives we have never had the type of relationship He had with David and the other prophets. The difference is the anointing that was on these people was a special anointing that we do not see anymore in today's world. That was part of God's process of writing the Bible. He used the prophets and others to do that. However, once that process was completed, we are directed to seek His voice by reading the Bible.

Thus, while God continues to communicate with us, He now does it in a different way. He communicates with us through the Bible. Read your Bible, and it will give you an answer to your problem or situation.

Today, there are people who get revelations in their sleep. Generally speaking, most do not understand or remember every detail about their dream. In addition, people also have difficulty interpreting their dreams/ revelations to make them reliable. This is not universal.

Some people today get revelations that turn out to be prophetic; therefore, there is a lot in this chapter we can take to heart, including the fact that we need to worship Him irrespective of our circumstances.

---

[95] Jeremiah 23:25-26

Whether we are going through trials and tribulations, we need to continue to worship Him.

In our church, we notice that many people come to us because they are facing a problem and come to the realization that they need prayers. Our corporate prayers involve these types of cases. The Bible asks us to find the lost and equip the found. We equip the found by teaching them how to surrender their personal pride and trust God in everything. We find that the bigger the problem that forces them to come to Jesus, the more readily they are to accept and obey Jesus. As a rule, people are more receptive at these times of distress than when everything in their lives is nice and rosy.

Pastor Rick Warren addresses another issue in this chapter that I consider paramount in my Christian journey. He says, "The common mistake Christians make in worship today is seeking an experience rather than seeking God. They look for a feeling, and if it happens they conclude that they have worshipped."

I am afraid I am one of those Christians who not only look for a feeling but actually expect it. I consider the Holy Spirit manifesting in me a necessary part of my praying experience, and this should remain the mainstay for all Pentecostals. The Pastor, being a Southern Baptist, can be excused for his views on this matter.

For me, before I pray for anyone, I feel more assured that God is doing His work through me when the Holy Spirit manifests His presence in me first. In fact, there is a prayer line I have borrowed from Elisha Goodman that I use often before I pray for anyone. It goes: "As I go into prayer, I pray that you will manifest your presence in my life."

The following passage from the Bible helps validate Jesus Christ, the original Apostles, and the Pentecost for me; and I hope for every Christian as well. God says, *"If you love me, keep my commands. And I will ask the Father, and he will give you another advocate to help you and be with you forever—the Spirit of truth. The world cannot accept him, because it neither sees him nor knows him. But you know him, for he lives with you and will be in you. I will not leave you as orphans; I will come to you."*[96]

The Lord Jesus goes on to identify the comforter as none other than the Holy Spirit. That verse says, *"But the Advocate, the Holy Spirit, whom*

---

[96]   John 14:15-18

the Father will send in my name, will teach you all things and will remind you of everything I have said to you."[97]

On Pentecost, the promise of a comforter became a reality for the disciples and all who were with them, and we read in the Bible which says, *"When the day of Pentecost came, they were all together in one place. Suddenly a sound like the blowing of a violent wind came from heaven and filled the whole house where they were sitting. They saw what seemed to be tongues of fire that separated and came to rest on each of them. All of them were filled with the Holy Spirit and began to speak in other tongues as the Spirit enabled them."*[98]

These are the verses that make Jesus Christ real for me. For many years, I lived my life according to the flesh. I did not read or need the Bible even though I was born into a Christian family. My mother's family was raised by missionaries, and my aunt, Kate Sukuta, celebrates that experience in her book, *Precious Mt. Silinda.* My father was also educated by the same mission schools, and later in life, in addition to his regular job as the chief instructor at a government experimental farming school, he became an ordained minister of the African Methodist Episcopal Church.

However, none of these influences stayed with me from before my teenage years. These were the years when Zimbabwe was fighting for independence from Britain, and there was a general distrust of Christianity. There was a general return to our traditional belief system that was characterized by worshipping our spirit elders. The practices followed were very similar to those of the Old Testament. The big difference being that Africans see their dead elders as spirit guardians who can bless or curse, depending on whether we are pleasing them or displeasing them in our daily lives. When we angered them we atoned for our misdeeds by sacrificing an animal. These were blood offerings similar to those in the Old Testament.

My next encounter with the Bible was after I married my second wife. She read the Bible often. There were times when I regarded her with ridicule because she carried the Bible to bed and read it whenever she was down. I could not understand her reliance on the Bible, and I had never owned a Bible of my own in my life. Yet when God decided it was time

---

[97] John 14:26

[98] Acts 2:1-4

for me to recognize Him as my Lord and Savior and to depend on Him for everything, the Bible became my closest ally. My old world quickly melted away, and a new one emerged with such drama I could not miss God's message. I converted, and I was saved. Once I made the decision, I did not waste much time getting baptized. I became an official of my new church, an offshoot of a larger worldwide organization based in the UK.

Within months of my conversion, I started feeling unfamiliar sensations each time I prayed. These were sensations I was previously unfamiliar with. As I continued to pray, read, and study the Bible, these sensations continued to grow until I started to expect them each time I prayed in earnest.

A year later, I was praying while exercising on the treadmill at home when I began speaking in tongues. It came just like that. To me, the language sounded Japanese, or one of those oriental languages. The experience was scary at first because it sounded like I was cursing somebody.

Thus, the very things that Jesus had said would happen to His disciples, and all believers 2,000 years ago were now happening to me. I was barely two years into my Christian journey when this happened.

Now the scriptures teach that everyone who accepts Jesus as Lord and Savior over their life receives the Holy Spirit. This does not mean they are spirit filled. In fact, one receives the spirit without any transformation taking place at all in the new Christian. It is the Holy Spirit that begins the transformation process, and these transformations have a lot to do with the soul as opposed to the spirit.

When one starts to change their bad habits, and they stop living according to the flesh, that is when they begin the process of transformation that happens from the inside. This is something that is a critical part of the process of becoming a Christian. It does not happen overnight and continues to the very day we die.

In today's church, there is de-emphasis of this wonderful Christian experience. There are many established Christian churches, including the mighty Catholic Church itself that look with disdain on the Charismatic Movement because they no longer have a place for the spirit-filled Christian. Pentecostals, on the other hand, encourage followers of Jesus being spirit filled. Some even value praying in tongues above praying in our own languages.

Right or wrong, I believe what was good for the Apostles the immediate successors of Jesus Christ is also good for me, and I thank God for that spiritual gift. I believe I am spirit filled when the Holy Spirit manifests His presence in me, and I speak in tongues.

There is another benefit of being spirit filled. The Bible says, *"In the same way, the Spirit helps us in our weakness. We do not know what we ought to pray for, but the Spirit himself intercedes for us through wordless groans. And he who searches our hearts knows the mind of the Spirit, because the Spirit intercedes for God's people in accordance with the will of God."*[99]

The question that is never fully answered is whether the devil can produce these same manifestations in a Christian, so when one believes they are spirit filled, it is actually the devil manifesting. Remember, the devil knows more about these things than we do. The hope is when we pray in the name of Jesus, the devil stays away.

Pastor Rick Warren appears to concede the point at the bottom of page 111 when he says, "God's omnipresence and the manifestation of his presence are two different things. One is a fact; the other is often a feeling." Yet from what Pastor Rick Warren says, I get the impression that it is not a common Christian experience to be spirit filled. One understands that not everyone is given the spiritual gift of speaking in tongues. That leaves me to ask the question: What is the validating event in your walk with Christ if the Holy Spirit does not manifest Himself in your life?

POINTS TO PONDER

Do you constantly hear "God told me to tell you . . ."?
How do you react to these messages?
Do they translate into reality?
Do you compare whether God's message through these channels conforms to the relevant Bible messages?

Scripture: Jeremiah 23

---

[99]   Romans 8:26-27

Purpose #2

YOU ARE FORMED
FOR GOD'S FAMILY

(Warren's Day 15-21)

Purpose No. 2 is a subset of my Purpose #4: Seeking God. It is the God connection, and given that the only organization God left here on earth is His church belonging to a church is a requirement.

CHAPTER 17

Formed for God's Family

(Warren's Day 15)

We are told in this part of the Pastor's book that we were formed for God's family. Because God is love, He treasures relationships and that the Trinity is His relationship with Himself. He also treasures a relationship with us, and the church is that relationship.

Purpose #2 as a whole deals with our quest for eternity. We have already established that we start our personal journey with Jesus when we are born again. This happens at the point in life when one decides to accept Jesus as Lord and Savior. Children born into the church generally take this step much earlier than children born to nonbelievers.

We have also established that for many, by the time they seek a connection with Jesus, they already have their real lives under way. They have things that drive their lives in place and that most of these drivers are related to their family responsibilities. They also have a purpose for living, or at least they think they do.

What we lack before we turn to Christ is a spiritual dimension. Typically, people seek God at various points in their life, and when they are born again, they simply rearrange their purposes and the things that drive their lives to conform them to a Christian lifestyle. That is if there is going to be any spiritual growth in them at all?

For many, this is as far as their spiritual growth will go. They have accepted Jesus as their Lord and Savior, but they continue in their sinful ways. According to the Christian Bible, it's not clear what the status of these folk is beyond the fact that they are saved. Does being saved translate into eternity? What happens to a believer who continues to sin? Apart from Romans 6:1 that addresses this issue, I am not sure anyone really knows the exact answer to this question.

For yet another group, their lifestyles have already been conformed to a Christian lifestyle by the time they are born again. Most children born into the church might be in this category. In my own case, though born into a third-generation Christian family—yes, on both sides of my family: my grandparents on both sides of my family were Christians—I did not stay in the faith for the better part of my adult life. My physical family made sure I went to church and taught me the little I knew about the Bible. They instilled in me the fear of God by emphasizing the Satan factor. It was drilled into us that those who disobey will end up in Gehenna, where people burn eternally.

I remember accepting Jesus at an early age. I mean, I could have been as young as eight or nine. I would be lying if I said I understood what it meant to be saved. I did not even know that it meant I had to conform my life to any particular Christian lifestyle. Whatever happened on the day of my conversion, therefore, was an isolated event that meant nothing to me. It definitely had no impact on my behavior. In biblical terms, I was not at an age when I could make a credible profession of the faith.

This brings us to the question at what age should children convert and be born again. The Bible offers no age requirement for one to be baptized into Christ, but it is generally agreed that the child must have a credible profession of faith when they make that decision. The phrase *a credible profession of faith* has Catholic Church beginnings and, therefore, is not exactly biblical. However, it is safe to say there is indeed an age when a child is too young to have a credible understanding of what it means to accept Jesus as Lord and Savior and be baptized into Jesus Christ.

With this background in mind, it was no wonder to me that, in reading chapter 15, the idea that one's spiritual family was more important than one's natural family immediately jumped at me. While my church family is important to me, it is superimposed on my physical family. The proposition that our spiritual families are more important than our natural families is difficult to digest. A look at the verse that says, *"If anyone does not provide for his relatives, and especially for his immediate family, he has denied the faith and is worse than an unbeliever"*[100] seems to suggest otherwise. It suggests that the care of our physical families is a prerequisite for becoming a member of the faith in the first place. It is a verse that speaks for itself.

That means if one puts God first to the exclusion of your family, your quest for eternity is pointless. The correct way to view this is to say loving your family first is an act of loving God and putting Him first. The two are on different dimensions and an "either or" approach will not work. We are required to do both and do them at the same time because one finds expression in the other. We should get our cue from that other verse that says, *"If you love me, keep my commands."*[101] The evidence that you love Him is found in your obedience. Therefore, there should be no conflict there.

I know those who advocate the view that God's family takes precedence over our physical families can quote Bible verses to support their viewpoint. They will quote the verse that says, *"If anyone comes to me and does not hate (rabbinical phrase, meaning to love less) his father and mother, wife and children, brothers and sisters, yes, and his own life also, he cannot be my disciple. And whoever does not bear his cross and come after me cannot be my disciple. So likewise, whoever of you does not forsake all that he has cannot be my disciple."*[102]

The same sentiments are expressed in the verse that says, *"Then Jesus said to His disciples, 'If anyone desires to come after me, let him deny himself, and take up his cross, and follow me. For whoever desires to save his life will lose it, but whoever loses his life for my sake will find it. For what profit is it to a man if he gains the whole world, and loses his own soul? Or what will a man give in exchange for his soul?'"*[103]

When these passages are quoted without context, they can mislead the reader into believing Jesus was putting the church ahead of family.

---

[100] 1 Timothy 5:8

[101] John 14:15

[102] Luke 14:26-27, 33

[103] Matthew 16:24-26

These verses were directed primarily at His disciples, meaning the twelve. These were the special people He invited to be the fishers of men at the beginning of His ministry. During the three years of His ministry, these people did put the church ahead of family. That same tradition is seen in the Catholic Church that has similar practices. You give your life to God in the literary sense. You forsake everything else for the Lord. Catholic nuns do just that.

Jesus also referred to His followers as disciples depending on the context. He did not expect all believers to be His disciples in the same sense as the twelve. We know this to be a fact because we are aware for instance that He had friends like Joseph, his two sisters Mary and Martha, and Nicodemus to name but a few. We do not read anywhere in the scriptures that there was any pressure or expectation that these people should abandon their lives and follow Jesus.

On the other hand, in the Great Commission, Jesus says clearly, *"Therefore go and make disciples of all nations, baptizing them in the name of the Father and of the Son and of the Holy Spirit, and teaching them to obey everything I have commanded you. And surely I am with you always, to the very end of the age."*[104] Here, it seems everyone who accepts Jesus as Lord and Savior becomes a disciple of Jesus. In this sense disciple, believer, and follower are synonymous. In the first two passages quoted on the other hand, Jesus was talking about his disciples while in the third he seems to be talking about his followers.

If we interpret these verses in this way, everything falls back into place. It also brings into sharp focus another dimension in "Jesuspeak." Jesus did not place much importance on life here on earth. He was not of this world. His view was if death came because one was a believer and got stoned for that reason, Jesus never focused on the loss of life but on the life that awaited the victim in heaven.

However, that is not our mindset here on earth. God has given us a lifetime, and we seek to maximize it. Life on earth is a complete experience in and of itself. Death is the end of life as we know it, and we need to operate within those God-given boundaries. We are born, and we die. Period. It is how we live this life that determines whether we will have everlasting life or damnation.

---

[104] Matthew 28:19

During our lifetime, loving one's family and putting them first is paramount. It is a prerequisite to putting God first. If this confuses you, welcome to "Godspeak." The God element in our lives runs along a parallel universe to ours, yet it has complete access to us. On the other hand, we have only limited access to the God universe, and the little that He has revealed to us confuses us because it sometimes does not fit with what we think we know. When you start to feel that way, just remember His thoughts are not your thoughts.

The confusion created here stems from treating one's lifetime here on earth and eternity as though they were one and the same thing. If we take it on authority that unbelievers will not go to heaven, the person who neglects his/her family does not stand a chance when it comes to eternity. The lesson here seems to be "Charity begins at home."

Another element of scripture that is often neglected in many discussions about God's hidden secrets is the possibility that some things we find in the Bible are intended to discipline us, to keep us on the straight and narrow. We all want so desperately to avoid spending eternity in Gehenna (translated hell) because, honestly, the graphic descriptions of that place are horrendous and scary. That might be one reason God has planted eternity into our hearts so we will not misbehave and find out His secrets. What might those secrets be?

If you think I am making this stuff up, look up the verse that says, *"What do workers gain from their toil? I have seen the burden God has laid on the human race. He has made everything beautiful in its time. He has also set eternity in the human heart; yet no one can fathom what God has done from beginning to end. I know that there is nothing better for people than to be happy and to do good while they live. That each of them may eat and drink, and find satisfaction in all their toil—this is the gift of God. I know that everything God does will endure forever; nothing can be added to it and nothing taken from it. God does it so that people will fear him."*[105]

I am not going to try and interpret the above passage because I have no clue what King Solomon was talking about. All I am doing is ask the question: Could it possibly mean this whole idea of eternity was planted into our hearts for one of God's purposes, and if so, what are the implications? There are several hints in the Bible about this and one of them is "the dead have no memory."

---

[105] Ecclesiastes 3:9-14

Before we leave the subject, let's take a look at another Bible passage that says, *"I also said to myself, 'As for humans, God tests them so that they may see that they are like the animals. Surely the fate of human beings is like that of the animals; the same fate awaits them both: As one dies, so dies the other. All have the same breath; humans have no advantage over animals. Everything is meaningless. All go to the same place; all come from dust, and to dust all return. Who knows if the human spirit rises upward and if the spirit of the animal goes down into the earth? So I saw that there is nothing better for a person than to enjoy their work, because that is their lot. For who can bring them to see what will happen after them?'"*[106]

These are the words of a prophet, and if he raises the possibility that our fate might be the same as the fate of animals, that, like animals, when we die that might be the end. Why, therefore, are so many religious leaders so hung-up on this heaven and hell stuff?

The answer is simple.

God left the issue deliberately vague for reasons only best known to Him. The subject of death and eternity is part of the hidden truths God simply does not want us to know everything there is to know. As I pointed out in other parts of this book, what would have happened had God not hidden the following information from us:

- The date of Jesus's return;
- Why does his fire (in hell) burn without destroying or reducing to ashes?
- If God is love, why deal so cruelly with sinners in hell?
- What is His exact relationship with Satan?
- Why did He allow Satan to tempt Him once He became flesh?
- Why not rid the world of Satan and his agents once and for all?
- Where exactly is heaven located in the universe?
- Why did he let people live the way they did in Jesus's time when the quality of life, communications, etc., could have been as we know it today?
- If the dead are really dead and remain dead until Jesus returns, who is currently up there in heaven, and how did they get there?

One could also ask why we need Jesus. The reason is because God has planted eternity in our hearts. We come to Jesus because we are told

---

[106] Ecclesiastes 3:18-22

He is the only way to the Father. His precious blood protects us from the evil one. We do not want the enemy, Satan, coming in and stealing our blessings even as we navigate this tortuous journey through this life here on earth. Then when everything is said and done, the only real incentive for obedience is our fear of damnation (going to hell).

We are constantly told not to focus on the things that really make us happy in this life because they are pleasures of the flesh. We are instead told to exercise self-control and focus on what we need to do to live on into eternity. That is the message that runs right through the Pastor's book. It is like a time-out from life so we can worship the Almighty God. However, the real message is do whatever it is you're doing right now and and live every minute of your life the way you want, but do it in obedience to God.

It is no wonder that most Christians constantly worry about the afterlife and whether or not they truly belong to His permanent family—the one we call God's family. I take the view that the church should be teaching us to enjoy what God has given us in this life and that if we do that in obedience to God in this life, we automatically belong into God's family now and forever.

POINTS TO PONDER

If we define biblical truths as things in the Bible for which we have no evidence or that seem to contradict our knowledge or earthly experiences, can you list them?
Apostle John believed the end times were coming in his lifetime (first century AD). Was he mistaken?
Was this a false prophecy?
Was this a biblical truth?

Scriptures: Luke 14:26-27, 33
                Ecclesiastes 3:18-22

CHARTER 18

Formed for God's Family

(Warren's Day 15 Cont'd)

When we are born again, we are born into this spiritual family.
Baptism is the means by which we identify with God's family.
Belonging to God's family is, therefore, life's greatest privilege.

In reading through this chapter, other ideas flood through one's mind on issues related to the idea of God's family. It is biblical, and the Apostles constantly refer to it in their writings. I have always believed that, whenever I talk about church and my membership in a church, I include my immediate family, especially the wife and children. Typically, people come to church as a family. When I say I am a member of God's family, I include my immediate family in that statement. The debate that follows is therefore an awakening for me.

GOD'S FAMILY vs. OUR NATURAL FAMILIES

The modern church views our natural family as the "first church." It is every young person's spiritual and physical survival kit. This is the first place where we learn about God, heaven, and hell. The people who surround us at birth and nurture us in those early years are our survival kit.

It is only later that we are exposed to other people at church or in day care. The bonds with this natural family are never broken. At what age does a child really outgrow this first family?

If we look at our suggested scheme or life cycle, the earliest this separation can occur is eighteen years. It might occur earlier in other cultures, but in Western cultures, it is eighteen or later. In America, where children are in college until twenty-two or later, this original family remains until one marries and starts their own family.

Ties to God's family, on the other hand, depend on the Christian habits of the family and the individual. They might weaken somewhat when one starts their own family. Therefore, when does the church family supersede this first family here on earth?

For most of us, this does not and will not happen in this lifetime. An important thing to note in this connection is we are members of our church families together with our physical families. That suggests that the two families are in a sense one and the same thing if one is in Christ because, by definition, you cannot love your church family if you do not love your natural family. God tells us this *when He says, "Whoever claims to love God yet hates a brother or sister is a liar. For whoever does not love their brother and sister whom they have seen, cannot love God, whom they have not seen. And he has given us this command: Anyone who loves God must also love their brother and sister."*[107]

There might be overlap or a suggestion of a conflict between the above verse and what Jesus called the greatest commandment of all which is to *"love the Lord your God with all your heart and with all your soul and with all your mind. This is the first and greatest commandment. And the second is like it: 'Love your neighbor as yourself.' All the Law and the Prophets hang on these two commandments."*[108]

One has to admit that the Bible makes no mention of our natural families as the "first church" as such. This is simply a descriptive characterization of the role of the natural family in our spiritual journey. In as far as our belonging to our natural families concurrently with our God family, the church, there should be no conflict, especially when viewed in context. The characteristics or spiritual habits one needs to develop once one is born again are best acquired through this Jesus

---

[107] John 4:20-21

[108]

connection, which is the church. Clearly, since the Pastor's book deals primarily with this aspect of our lives and failed to make that clear in his original message, the apparent conflict is not surprising, but it is not real.

Once we exit this world at death, God's family does take precedence, even though there is nothing [don't quote me] in the scriptures that says our church buddies will be our buddies in heaven, just as there is nothing that says we will be with our natural families in heaven.

I can buy the proposition that the church as we know it helps strengthen the "first church" and reinforce it here on earth. We encourage members of the "first church" to come to church with us. The expectation is of course that they will all end up in heaven if they obey God's commands. These are the people you share your ups and downs with here on earth. The transition from this life to the next should be seamless. Therefore, you should enjoy this life and continue into the next without losing a single beat. The only thing that will stop this from happening is your sin, and the only focus should be on avoiding sin and not to live constrained and confined lives. People should not live in fear of everything they enjoy.

The rules are simple: live your life in obedience to God.

DEFINING GOD'S RICHES

A second issue that emerges for me in going through this chapter of the Pastor's book is that he quotes the verse that says, *"And my God will meet all your needs according to the riches of his glory in Christ Jesus."*[109] He lists for us what these riches comprise of. They are his grace, kindness, patience, glory, wisdom, power, and mercy. He omits any reference to material riches even though the context we normally associate the word *riches* is material riches.

When we go to the actual context of the quoted verse in the Bible, the Apostle Paul was talking about material giving. He had received material gifts from the Philippians and was blessing the Philippians and wishing that God would bless them by supplying all their needs according to His riches in glory in Christ Jesus. He was clearly referring to the need to enhance their ability to give.

---

[109] Philippians 4:19

In the verses preceding this verse, the Apostle's context is clear when he says, *"Moreover, as you Philippians know, in the early days of your acquaintance with the gospel, when I set out from Macedonia, not one church shared with me in the matter of giving and receiving, except you only; for even when I was in Thessalonica, you sent me aid more than once when I was in need. Not that I desire your gifts; what I desire is that more be credited to your account. I have received full payment and have more than enough. I am amply supplied, now that I have received from Epaphroditus the gifts you sent. They are a fragrant offering, an acceptable sacrifice, pleasing to God."*[110]

It is not clear how the Pastor managed to give an interpretation that was entirely spiritual when the giving involved in the case of the Philippians was material. I am sure there is a reasonable explanation to this, but without that clarification, this creates confusion in the minds of most readers.

As church leaders, we encourage giving of all kinds, and most of it is material giving. Clearly, in thanking the saints, for giving we use the Apostle's words and say, "May the Lord meet all your needs according to his riches in glory in Christ Jesus." By that, we include material riches for it is from that source that they are able to give more.

A similar problem follows the discussion on inheritance.

The tendency to confine definitions and meanings of commonly used words to the hereafter continues to plague the book. The Pastor's book should give us context within our present lives and then project the benefits to the hereafter. The Bible says, *"A good man leaves an inheritance for his children but a sinners wealth is stored up for the righteous."*[111] The same discussion carried out within the context of this verse yields a completely different conclusion.

The Pastor instead quotes Ephesians 1:18, and he discusses that in the same abstract terms completely ignoring the other meanings of inheritance that pertain to this life. His readers are of this world, and while they would like to learn about the inheritance in heaven if they make it there, they also want to know of the benefits they stand to gain here on earth by amassing wealth in obedience to God. If God thought untold wealth was good for Abraham, Solomon, Job, and the rest of His friends, who are we to teach that wealth is not good for the rest of us?

---

[110] Philippians 4:15-18
[111] Proverbs 13:22

The Pastor even has some words to say about retirement as a goal. For those of us who continue to afford to pay our tithes and offerings from our retirement income, not preparing for retirement is imprudent, and the Bible teaches prudence. As church leaders, we cannot afford to teach or infuse into people's mind ideas that are imprudent in this life, for this life on earth is a complete experience in and of itself. The teaching that says your rewards are in heaven is not very useful though a biblical truth.

In fact, the message at page 119 directly contradicts the quotation he uses on the same page that says, *"Whatever you do work at it with all your heart, as working for the Lord, not for men since you know that you will receive an inheritance from the Lord as a reward."*[112]

Clearly, what we do on earth is the necessary preparation for eternity, if indeed there is eternity. Emphasis should be on our earthly lives not only because this is reality but also because, if we fail here on earth, we are almost guaranteed to fail in heaven. Above all, we should always be reminded that there are no black and white answers when it comes to God. There are simply plenty shades of grey.

POINTS TO PONDER

What is your exact relationship with the people you fellowship with?
How does it compare with your relationship with your family?
What obligations do you have to the people you fellowship with?
Do you expect them to share responsibility for raising your children?
List all the responsibilities you have for members of you household.
In what sense might your church family be more important to you than your natural family?

Scriptures: Ecclesiastes 3:9-11
                Ecclesiastes 3:18-22

---

[112]   Colossians 3:23-24

CHAPTER 19

What Matters Most

(Warren's Day 16)

This chapter is about love. We are told that the best use of life is to love and that love will last forever. The author tells us we will be evaluated on our love, and that the best time to love is now.

This chapter to me continues the same "disconnect" of the previous chapter. According to the author, the emphasis in our lives should not be on our natural families. He quotes the following verse that says, *"Therefore, as we have opportunity, let us do good to all people, especially to those who belong to the family of believers."*[113]

I always read the same verse as meaning that believers, together with their families, should do good to all people, especially to those who belong to the family of believers. I always made the assumption that parents and their children are one until the children come of age and start their own family unit. When God asked Abraham to move away from his native land to a land God had appointed for him, there was no need for God to specify that he was to move together with his household. It is understood that a person is one with his household.

---

[113]   Galatians 6:10

The Pastor in this chapter appears to be only vaguely aware of the distinctions that need to be made here. On page 126, he says some of us act as though relationships are something to be squeezed into our schedule. He says we talk about finding time for our children or making time for people in our lives. The truth is we love our children all the time by being there for them always. Even when we are physically absent, we are there for them because we accept responsibility for their well-being; and in this age of technology, we keep in touch with them either by telephone or via the Internet when we are not physically present.

Typically, in our daily lives, when we wake up, each has a responsibility to attend to. After breakfast, Daddy and Mommy go to work, while the children go to school. We have put into place mechanisms that assure that our children are safe and occupied while we are at work. There is nothing wrong with these schedules that are part of our need to survive and to provide for our families. Providing for one's household is a responsibility imposed on us by God. Ordinarily, we do not carry out these basic responsibilities for other believers (households), unless we become aware of a "lack" on the part of the other believer, and we are in a position to help. In such cases, God wants us to step in and offer help in accordance with our means.

Life is, however, an integrated process, and it involves being busy in order to feed our families. It involves paying bills, and when you cannot pay your bills, your capacity to help your neighbor is also diminished. This integrated whole includes loving your neighbor as well. There is nothing wrong with a hardworking fellow who wants to use his excess wealth to build schools and hospitals and help the poor.

We live in a world where we see this happening before our very own eyes. Bill Gates and Warren Buffet are examples of people who are doing exactly that. Do they love less because they are focusing on these other things in their lives? There is no doubt that these are busy people and that they devote an inordinate amount of time away from mundane family matters. However, because of their wealth, they have created other mechanisms to make up for their lack of time. They do not personally have to walk the child to the school's bus stop. They have most probably employed someone else to do that or to drive and pick up kids from school. We should, therefore, be celebrating these folks for what they do.

The problem with humanity today is we find it difficult to identify the boundaries to our knowledge of and about God. Instead of admitting that we do not always know what God intended in any given situation, we provide answers that do not completely dovetail with what we already know about God. We tend to search the Bible for the verses that will back up our own interpretations of the situation, even where there are verses that tend to confirm a contrary point of view.

Let us answer some of these questions for example. Who gives us wealth? The Bible tells us to *"remember the LORD your God, for it is he who gives you power to get wealth that he may confirm his covenant that he swore to your fathers, as it is this day."*[114] If it is God who does this, then why does He give to believers and nonbelievers alike? The truth is we do not know the answer to that question. Christians will offer a myriad of answers to the question.

The answer might be that, in His eyes, we are all His children and that the issue of wealth is not a variable in the general scheme of things. He offers to all His children alike based on a criteria only He knows. It is like a father who has two children—one of them obedient while the other is disobedient. The father does not deny the disobedient child food and shelter. He continues to provide for both children while at the same time taking other measures to bring the disobedient child in line.

In "Biblespeak," when we ask this question, we might be asking amiss. There are many areas in the Bible where God's position is left vague. A good example is why should we confess our sins daily when God has already forgiven all our past, present, and future sins? Be warned in this case that God never said that our sins—past, present, and future— were forgiven. We infer that position from reading a number of other verses that tend to draw us to that conclusion.

One of those verses is the one that says, *"He forgave us all our sins."*[115] If this is accurate, then the conventional answer we get when we ask this question is correct. That answer is based on the verse that says, *"If we confess our sins, he is faithful and just and will forgive us our sins and purify us from all unrighteousness."*[116] It says when we sin after we have accepted Jesus as our Lord and Savior, we interfere with our fellowship with God. Therefore, we need to acknowledge (confess) our mistakes to Him in order to restore our fellowship with Him.

---

[114] Deuteronomy 8:18

[115] Colossians 2:13

[116] 1 John 1:9

Note, however, that this answer is predicated on the correctness of our previous answer. If for any reason only our past sins are forgiven, then we would need to continue to confess with respect to our present and future sins in accordance with 1 John 1:9.

There are many verses in this category including the issue of tithes. The New Testament simply says God loves a cheerful giver, while the Old Testament, which is the nearest thing to the Jewish Torah, is more precise on the issue. One has to read everything about tithing for themselves and settle for a position they are personally comfortable with. You cannot rely entirely on the church on such matters because the church has a personal interest in the matter. It survives on tithes and offerings.

Another verse that boggles the mind on the issue of sin is the one that asks, *"What shall we say, then? Shall we go on sinning so that grace may increase?"*[117] That verse and the explanation that follows suggests that believers are not expected to continue sinning (willfully) and that at some point, grace "evaporates for those who continue to sin." The Bible tells us that *"if we deliberately keep on sinning after we have received the knowledge of the truth, no sacrifice for sins is left, but only a fearful expectation of judgment and of raging fire that will consume the enemies of God."*[118]

This suggests that if we continue to sin due to our sinful nature, we might lose the saving grace that was freely given by the death of Christ. There are many vexing questions about life and Christianity for which mankind still has no answers. The result is a wealth of sometimes misleading interpretations. However, as usual, we never want to admit the truth that we do not know everything about God other than what He has chosen to reveal to us. We like instead to pretend we have the answers when we really don't.

The other often-asked question is if God is in control, how come He allows disasters to happen? The truth is God is and remains a mystery. Those of us who have accepted Christianity should admit that we are doing so not so much because we understand everything about Him but because, given what we know, "we would rather live our lives as if there is a God and when we die, find out that there is no God, than live our lives as if there is no God and die only to find out that there is a God." Then

---

[117] Romans 6:1

[118] Hebrews 10:26

it will be too late to make amends. Maybe this has always been God's design.

This statement is an admission that we do not know enough about God, but on the basis of what we know, He offers the best way to live our lives.

Anyway, we are supposed to be talking about wealth. Pastor Warren says love leaves a legacy and how you treat people has a bigger impact than wealth and accomplishments. He immediately mentions Mother Teresa. Her work sure impacted the world, but so did Henry Ford and Thomas Edison. These folks spent countless hours working at their craft, and the result is that mankind benefitted from their work. The real issue in God's eyes is not so much their wealth or accomplishments, but whether they accomplished what they accomplished in obedience to God.

It is easier to say yes with respect to Mother Teresa because of the nature of her work than the other two, but God blessed these titans of the industry so they in turn could bless us. It is possible that my confusion here stems from the fact that I have assumed that God blesses only those He approves. The truth could be God sometimes blesses even those He does not approve for reasons only known to Him.

The Pastor also discusses relationships. His discourse about relationships on page 126 is true and accurate. While relationships are important, not all relationships matter at death's door. It is that "first church" relationship that seems to count the most. In most reports about death, we hear that he/she was surrounded by his/her family. The second family relationship usually takes a secondary position in one's final days. They do come around to bury the dead, but members of the "first church" carry the larger burden of the grieving. It is thus possible for religious writers like Pastor Rick Warren to inspire others with their thoughts, even where those thoughts when put under the microscope show amazing gaps in logic.

The book talks about learning to love as though it is one and the same thing as learning to drive a car or ride a bicycle. Love is a qualitative thing that we can never fully grasp. That is why the Bible helps us identify love's various elements as follows:

> Love is patient, love is kind. It does not envy, it does not boast, it is not proud. It does not dishonor others, it is not self-seeking, it is not easily angered, it keeps no record of wrongs.

> Love does not delight in evil but rejoices with the truth. It always protects, always trusts, always hopes, always perseveres. Love never fails. But where there are prophecies, they will cease; where there are tongues, they will be stilled; where there is knowledge, it will pass away. For we know in part and we prophesy in part, but when completeness comes, what is in part disappears. When I was a child, I talked like a child, I thought like a child, I reasoned like a child. When I became a man, I put the ways of childhood behind me. For now we see only a reflection as in a mirror; then we shall see face to face. Now I know in part; then I shall know fully, even as I am fully known. And now these three remain: faith, hope and love. But the greatest of these is love.[119]

The problem is, love is internal, and whether we are loving or simply showing off depends on one's motivation for the act of love that they are showing to another. I agree with the author that love is how you treat others. A married person who prays, goes to church, and considers himself/herself loving but routinely denies conjugal rights to the spouse is clearly unloving in the context of a marriage. These types of people see love through their own eyes. If they were mature, they would realize that what started off as a loving relationship has been turned into a bed of nails for the other person.

The Bible has anticipated many events in our lives. God asks, *"How can you say you love me when you do not love your own brother, someone you have seen?"*[120] How in hell can you please God when you cannot please even the person lying right next to you in bed?

Another way of looking at this teaching in a marriage situation is to constantly ask the question, "Am I pleasing my spouse?" If when he or she asks, the answer is no, you're clearly not pleasing her or him.

Sometimes though we want to please our partners, but other issues interfere. The trick is to explain this to your partner but keep them to a minimum. Yet the one area spouses falter the most is with sex. When a man or a woman strikes out four out of five times they approach the other for sex, that relationship is most likely doomed.

---

[119] 1 Corinthians 13:4-13

[120] 1 John 4:20

Movie makers like to capture this situation on film. The movie will capture the mood of an excited wife looking forward to having sex with her husband, and all he does is groan that he is tired, turns away, and quickly falls asleep. The wife remains wide awake, agonizing over the situation. Eventually, she gets up and goes to the kitchen to do the dishes or the laundry when just five minutes of loving attention would have allowed her to go to sleep and sleep just as soundly.

Now let's make the graphic even worse by first showing the same husband fornicating with his secretary before going home to the lonely wife. How do we feel now? I am not arguing that each time the husband or wife asks, they should get, but only to show how unloving we are even in love by not making "pleasing" the ones we love the byword of our marriages. If we can look back and judge ourselves by whether or not we are pleasing our better halves, we can then take that same test with our children, our parents, and then our neighbors. If you can answer "yes, yes, yes, yes," then we can see that all this is pleasing to God as well. That is obedience.

A believer who is in this situation does not need to do any other special act in order to show they put God first in everything they do. The taste is in the act of obeying God by what you do with the people around you. A word of caution though. Pleasing someone does not mean being a doormat. It is not the same thing as giving in to the other's unreasonable demands.

One should have sufficient wisdom to know that paying your neighbor's rent when you cannot pay your own rent definitely pleases your neighbor but can lead to ruin. Likewise, sleeping with your lonely neighbor, though pleasing to your neighbor, is not love. It is fornication and is not pleasing to God, so perish the thought.

One also doubts the proposition that time spent on anything shows a person's priorities. If my wife loves to spend time at the gym, and I like to play golf, and the kids have other priorities, I do not see how the time spent apart measures anything about the state of loving in our family. Today's world is very different from the world that existed when biblical people lived. We live in a world where some parents work away from home just to feed the family. That's love. Therefore, one needs to be sensitive to the conditions under which some of our fellow Christians operate when making some of these statements about love.

Within the context of American life, the division of labor in the home between husband and wife and between the home and the school are part of the love we shower on our children to make sure they grow into mature, educated and well-adjusted individuals, and fit to be good parents themselves when their time comes. That is our reality, and the church should operate within the context of that reality. That is if we agree that God's purposes for putting us here on earth were:

1. to be fruitful and increase in number;
2. to fill the world;
3. to take dominion over God's other creations;
4. to harness all that he has provided for our own welfare;
5. to take care of others around us; and
6. to seek a connection to God.

A purpose driven life will necessarily be guided by God's purposes for us, and His will for us will automatically align with his purposes. *"If anyone does not provide for his relatives, and especially for his immediate family, he has denied the faith and is worse than an unbeliever."*[121]

POINTS TO PONDER

What are your feelings about the idea God's family (the Church) is more important than our own natural families?

Do you believe time taken away from family in order to work is a negative reflection of the love the family units shares?

Who gives us the power to make wealth?

Why does God give wealth to believers and non-believers alike?

Scriptures: 1 Timothy 5:8
                   1 John 4:20
                   Deuteronomy 8:18

---

[121] 1 Timothy 5:8

CHAPTER 20

(Warren's Day 17 to 21)

In chapter 17, we learn that we all need a place to belong and that the church is just that place. Following Jesus is not just believing, but it also involves belonging. We are told about the benefits of the church family.

On Day 18, we learn that real fellowship is authentic, mutual, experiencing sympathy and mercy. On Days 19, 20 and 21, we learn about cultivating community, restoring broken fellowship, and protecting your church. Going through these five chapters, one begins to understand why the Pastor's book became such a runner away best seller. Pastor Warren dissects the church connection for believers in a way that's both real and clear. His message confirms much of what I have personally experienced in our own small church. It is about church membership and our role in the church. Anyone who has tried to run a church no matter how small will confirm a lot of the advice Pastor Rick Warren dishes out in these chapters.

We are told for instance that we need a place to belong (Day 17) and that we cannot fulfill God's purposes on our own. Typically, belonging to a church means belonging to a local church. We need a church family because that is what identifies us as believers in Christ.

We also learn that a church family will keep us from backsliding. I think we see this in our churches a lot. The church connection keeps you connected even during those times when you have lost your focus and have stopped going to church. Being a church member is an expression of commitment.

The Pastor then talks about experiencing life together as members of a local church (Day 18). We are reminded of God's promise that where two or more are gathered in His name, He will be there with us[122]. This is a significant promise because, just knowing that when two or more join together in prayer, God is present is huge for the Christian.

For those Christians in whom the Holy Ghost manifests when they pray, it is as though this promise is confirmed every time they join with others in prayer. I particularly found relevance in the discussion about fellowship being authentic. He says fellowship should be "genuine, heart to heart, sometimes gut level sharing. It happens when people are honest about who they are and what is happening in their lives. They share their hurts, reveal their feelings, confess their failures, disclose their doubts, admit their fears, acknowledge their weaknesses and ask for help and prayer."

Many of the things the Pastor has to say in this chapter are real to Christians who belong to a church because this is the life we live. We experience sympathy when we encounter a crisis from our fellow Christians. One can only but affirm statements regarding the need to forgive and to trust.

We are further told in this chapter that the church is the family of God. That is what the Apostle Paul says, *"Although I hope to come to you soon, I am writing you these instructions so that, if I am delayed, you will know how people ought to conduct themselves in God's household, which is the church of the living God, the pillar and foundation of the truth."*[123]

The Pastor says building community requires honesty, humility, and courtesy. He says it also requires confidentiality, and this can be a big problem in small churches where everybody knows everybody's business. What we find is that people will ask for prayers when they encounter problems in their lives. However, once the crisis has passed, they want everybody to forget about the issue they brought before the congregation.

That does not always happen, and we have had people leave the church for this reason alone. They will complain that someone is

---

[122]   Matthew 18:20

[123]   1 Timothy 3:14-15

gossiping about them when all they have done is follow up on an issue brought to the church by the very same person who is now complaining.

Another source of lack of confidentiality are testimonies. The scriptures tell us that *"they conquered by the blood of the lamb and the word of their testimonies."*[124] We encourage people to give a testimony about how God has intervened in their lives to resolve an issue. The whole congregation gets to know what has transpired, and it can lead to gossiping too. It is a problem that is difficult to control in any church.

The Pastor addresses these issues (page 151) by saying, "If you're a member of a small group or class, I urge you to make a group covenant that includes the nine characteristics of biblical fellowship: we will share our true feelings (authenticity), encourage each other (mutuality), support each other (sympathy), forgive each other (mercy), speak the truth in love (honesty), admit our weaknesses (humility), respect our differences (courtesy), not gossip (confidentiality), and make a group a priority (frequency)." Amen!

In chapter 20 we learn about restoring broken fellowship. We are told to value church relationships and maintain them. We are reminded that God wants us to be peacemakers and to settle our relationships with each other. Pastor Warren then gives us seven biblical steps for restoring fellowship (153-159). We are told to talk to God before talking to the person with whom we need to restore fellowship, take initiative and sympathize with their feelings, admit your part in the conflict, attack the problem and not the person. We are advised to cooperate and focus on reconciliation as opposed to resolution.

In chapter 21, the Pastor talks about protecting your church, and we are told it is our duty to protect the unity of your church. Anyone involved with a church cannot disagree with this statement. There are times when we know what a solution to a problem should be, but we prescribe instead a solution that maintains the unity of the church. We are advised to focus on the things we have in common and not on our differences. This is good advice to put out in any situation.

The author reminds us to have realistic expectations because there is a gap between the ideal and reality in this area. Each church has its own set of weaknesses and that is why one has to approach the problem with realistic expectations.

---

[124]   Revelation 12:11

The basic biblical advice in church conflict resolution is that *"if your brother or sister sins, go and point out their fault, just between the two of you. If they listen to you, you have won them over. But if they will not listen, take one or two others along, so that 'every matter may be established by the testimony of two or three witnesses.' If they still refuse to listen, tell it to the church; and if they refuse to listen even to the church, treat them as you would a pagan or a tax collector."*[125]

The Pastor concludes the chapter by advising that we support our pastors and church leaders. There are no perfect leaders out there, but we all need to lower our expectations.

POINTS TO PONDER

What should we say to people who claim they worship alone?
Is there an ideal sized church? I mean, can a church be so small it negates the whole idea of fellowshipping together?
What are the challenges of restoring broken fellowship?
How should we support our Pastors?
How do we protect our church?

Scriptures: John 17:21 (Jesus prays for unity in the church.)
                Acts 2:42 (Fellowship)
                John 13:34-35(Unity)

---

[125]   Matthew 18:15-17

Purpose #3

YOU WERE CREATED
TO BE LIKE CHRIST

Purpose No. 3 can be viewed as a legitimate purpose for our creation, even though it does not meet the basic requirements of the other purposes. God created us to serve His purpose, and we do that by fulfilling the role He wanted us to play in the grand scheme of things. Our being created in His likeness, while an honor, in and of itself does not serve a purpose.

CHAPTER 21

You Were Created to be Like Jesus

(Warren's Day 22)

In this chapter, we are told that we were created to be like Christ. The Pastor correctly emphasizes that we will never become God or even a god. We are told that God's ultimate goal is not comfort but character development. We are also told that Christians misinterpret Jesus's promise of an abundant life. God uses the Holy Spirit to produce in us a Christlike character. We must, therefore, cooperate with the Holy Spirit. God also uses His Word, people and circumstances to mold us.

Purpose #3 of Pastor Rick Warren's book is that we were created to be like Christ. This statement is about creation (think Adam and Eve), but the Pastor's book is about obedience to God as believers. That is part of the "disconnect" that I discern in his overall message. Yet this also happens to be the one purpose in his book that rings true. The reason is it is biblical.

God did create us in his own image and likeness.[126] The one issue I have raised from the beginning has been that the Pastor's five purposes should have been based on the purposes God gave when He created

---

[126] Genesis 1:26-27

human beings (Adam and Eve). God's exact words on the subject were that they should be fruitful; they should multiply and fill the world and take dominion of all His other creations on earth.

God had just created the heavens and the earth and was pleased with His creation. Now He wanted someone to inhabit the earth, and He came up with the brilliant idea of creating human beings in His own image. These would be His people, His creations. Therefore, He fully expected them to obey and worship Him, but that was not the reason why God placed us on this planet.

It is within this context that we learn that one of God's five reasons for our creation was to make us more like Jesus Christ. This is the type of statement that creates confusion if not properly explained. For starters at creation, Jesus Christ had not yet become flesh. He did not have a physical shape. That only happened several centuries after the creation of the heavens and the earth. To make this statement, one has to base it on God's foreknowledge of the future, which opens up a whole new area of discussion. In other words, what Pastor Rick Warren is saying is that God knew then that the devil would deceive Adam and Eve and that humankind would disobey him.

The reason we struggle with these concepts and ideas is we are never told what God included in the phrase "in our own image," and chances are nobody will ever know for sure. Nevertheless, we do know what God did not include in the phrase "in our own image." He did not pass on to us His godly powers as the Pastor correctly notes. He only wanted us to be godly.

We also know that Jesus was not conceived in sin, but we all were. The Bible tells us so. The actual verse says, *"Surely I was sinful at birth, sinful from the time my mother conceived me."*[127] Surely, there is something in the way we are conceived that marks us apart from Jesus. We are conceived when the male sperm is introduced into the woman's womb. Is this where our sinful nature comes from?

Our religious leaders rarely debate this issue. It raises of course the possibility that the forbidden fruit Adam and Eve ate included opening their eyes to the pleasures of sex between man and woman—something God had not intended them to know the way they got to know it. Nonetheless, our God is a God of infinite wisdom. The architecture of the

---

[127] Psalm 51:5

male and female reproductive organs leave no doubt they were designed for sex. If God had not intended for a man and a woman to become one flesh, He would not have designed us that way.

Yet when God wanted to become flesh, He avoided normal human conception. He did not want Joseph's sperm into Mary's womb. What was the reason for this? This is something that has never been fully explained and remains one of God's secrets. We refer to it as Immaculate Conception, and it is so because no male sperm was involved. God simply planted His son in Mary's womb while she was still a virgin.

Even though Jesus was God in the flesh, He never married. He never engaged in sexual relationships with a woman. He also did not have to deal with the challenges of being a husband and father. Again, our partaking in sex with a woman seems to mark us apart from Jesus (the Christian God). We are, therefore, unlike Him in this respect as well.

The Catholic Church, by insisting that its clergy not marry, seems to mirror this issue of sex between man and woman as a part of our fall from grace. These very relationships impact us differently in our way of relating to wife, husband, and family from the way someone without these ties relates to life.

We are told in the scriptures that Jesus knew no sin.[128] The same scriptures tell us that we all have sinned and fall short of the glory of God.[129] We, therefore, can never be sinless like Jesus. Our sin nature does mark us apart from Jesus. This leads to the question: What was it then about Christ Jesus that God wanted us to emulate?

Physically, He was all flesh and blood just like us, but that is hardly what God had in mind when He decided to create us in His own image. It was clearly His values, His character, His nature, and his sinless life that He wanted us to emulate.

How then are people like us born with a sinful nature supposed to become Christlike? Pastor Warren says God indeed has a physical likeness, and we see that in Jesus. This could be both fact and fiction. Jesus did tell His disciples that if you have seen me, you have seen the Father.[130] It is possible that Jesus was talking about God's physical appearance. Conventional wisdom suggests that He was talking about

---

[128] 2 Corinthians 5:21

[129] Romans 3:23

[130] John 14:7-9

God's nature and character for God is spirit. Therefore, He is without the human form ordinarily associated with humankind.

The theory that we were created to be like Jesus clearly has obvious limitations. We were never created to have all the attributes of God, neither is it accurate to argue that God passed all His attributes to us. If the fruits of the Spirit are love, joy, peace, forbearance, kindness, goodness, faithfulness, gentleness, and self-control, then much of that was not passed on to us either. We know that is the ideal God expects of us, but we have to struggle to develop these attributes. Because we live in this corrupted world, a community of unbelievers, it is doubtful we will ever come anywhere near that.

The wars we wage against each other, the greed we thrive on, and the strife we cause all mitigate against the attainment of these godly values. What we can all agree on is that Jesus is like a beacon of light, and we see Him as an ideal in whose direction we should aim our lives, but that is about all we will ever be.

Throughout history, we have been rebellious and sinful. In today's world, only 32 percent of humanity are professing Christians, which means two-thirds of humanity do not believe in Jesus Christ. Of the 32 percent who profess to be Christians, it is hard to estimate the percentage that live a Christian lifestyle, which means for many Christians, the cross and the grace of God are the only things that stand between them and damnation. This is simply a frightening situation for mankind if indeed there is a heaven and hell.

If God had created us to be like Jesus, He would have avoided some of the pitfalls into which we are born and made it a little easier for us to live joyful, peaceful lives. Jesus was a special case, and there is no doubt the world would be a better place if we were like Jesus.

That is different from the statement the Pastor makes that we were created to be like Jesus. Some of the things Jesus did were based on the fact that He knew much more about the Father, His nature, and His mindset than we do.

The two-thirds of humanity who do not believe in Jesus would change if they knew for sure that (1) there is life after death, (2) there is heaven and hell, and (3) the only way to the Father is through Jesus. That these Christian biblical truths have not been made manifest has surely contributed to the state of affairs we face.

HAVE LIFE AND HAVE IT MORE ABUNDANTLY

The Pastor also gives us an interpretation of John 10:10, especially that part where Jesus says He came so we can have life and have it more abundantly. He says Christians misinterpret Jesus's promise of an abundant life, and He happens to be correct.

The abundance in John 10:10 is indeed about eternity. It does not mean we will have perfect health, a comfortable lifestyle, or any of the other good things we associate with the good life here on earth. However, the fact that people misinterpret John 10:10 does not mean God does not want us to live the good life here on earth. There are other verses in the Bible that suggest that God does not want us to live in poverty and in sickness either.

Jesus's preoccupation with the widow, the orphan, and the poor is evidence that He was concerned about the disadvantaged. This has to be balanced with the reality that Jesus accepted slavery as a normal state of life for some people—something that begs an explanation. Did Jesus compromise His values for political reasons? Is slavery biblical? Was God discriminatory when He chose the Jews as His people ahead of everybody else? The Greeks and the Arabs were just as literate as the Jews, so why the Jews? These questions only go to show that we only have a glimpse of the character and nature of our Creator. He is manifestly a mystery.

God does bless people with material things. King Solomon, when asked what he wanted, responded that all he wanted was wisdom to rule God's people. God responded by saying, *"Since this is your heart's desire and you have not asked for wealth, possessions or honor, nor for the death of your enemies, and since you have not asked for a long life but for wisdom and knowledge to govern my people over whom I have made you king, therefore wisdom and knowledge will be given you. And I will also give you wealth, possessions and honor, such as no king who was before you ever had and none after you will have."*[131] God, therefore, gave Solomon untold riches.

Abrahams's eldest servant says to Rebekkah, the woman who was to become Isaac's future wife, *"The LORD has blessed my master abundantly, and he has become wealthy. He has given him sheep and cattle, silver and gold, male and female servants, and camels and donkeys."*[132]

---

[131] 1 Kings 3:11-13

[132] Genesis 24:35

These two verses tell us clearly that God's blessings include material wealth. Thus, if Christians have a mindset that says blessing equals rich, it clearly has its genesis in the Bible. The problem with our Creator is He has too many secrets. He has never revealed why, if all good things come from Him, He blesses both Christians (believers) and nonbelievers with riches alike.

Nobody has ever been able to explain this adequately to us.

The underappreciated truth might be that there are two kingdoms out there that mirror each other. We can get our material blessings from either kingdom. The difference is that *"the blessing of the LORD makes rich, and he adds no sorrow with it."*[133] This situation of two kingdoms is clearly demonstrated by Pharaoh's magicians being able to replicate everything Moses did. He turned his stick into a snake, and the magicians replicated. God demonstrated His supremacy by having Moses's snake devour the others.

The reverse is also true. God punishes by dispossessing and by allowing Satan to come steal, kill, and destroy. The notion that poverty (in material terms) is the reverse side of a blessing (in material terms) is also biblical. We should not blame people for thinking that poverty and other deprivations of this life are caused by the dark forces of this world and that they are curses. Because God has allowed that to happen, Christians, when plagued by these things, see this as punishment. The Bible, of course, says these are trials, tests, and tribulations.

Others also argue that the things we take for granted like the air we breathe, the water we drink, and the like are blessings from God. There is no doubt these are blessings, but general usage dictates that the blessings people pray for are those in Genesis 24:35 above. They will pray for water only when it is not freely available.

Pastor Rick Warren is incorrect when he says God does not want us to live in mansions. We know that He wants some of us to do exactly that as with King Solomon and King David and other rich people of the Bible if we have the means.

We can also look at this question from a different angle. We know God wants us to give to the poor. This means He expects those He has blessed with material things to bless those less fortunate than they are. There is nothing wrong or unbiblical for a Christian to work hard so he/

---

[133] Proverbs 10:22

she can make a lot of money that he/she then uses to bless (help) the poor. The problem comes when the accumulation of wealth becomes an end in itself. This is what we call idolatry. It is about hoarding.

There are situations where one keeps piling up the riches for the sake of accumulating wealth without any thought at all to helping those less fortunate. One suspects that this is common among today's rich people. If the tax laws in the USA did not allow a deduction for charitable giving, some of these folks might give nothing away except what they are forced to surrender to the taxman. Some die still trying to accumulate even more wealth. Others remain completely oblivious to the plight of the poor around them. Yet there is something satisfying about giving the little one has to help a fellow worshipper get over the hump.

A scripture that should benefit these Christians in this regard says, *"Give, and it will be given to you. A good measure, pressed down, shaken together and running over, will be poured into your lap. For with the measure you use, it will be measured to you."*[134] Allistair Kent, writing in WisdomOnWealth.Org., sees it the other way. We receive a blessing so we can give. In other words, we give what we already have; so to have means, we have already received. He says we abuse the principle here by giving (think tithes and offerings) so we can get (a breakthrough or material abundance), when what we should be doing is getting (a blessing) so we can (give) bless others with what we have been given.

Therefore, the misuse of John 10:10 does not negate the fact that we expect blessings in both material and spiritual things. Rather than discourage people's expectations in this area, we should give them the right Bible verses to use. We go back to the old standby that says, *"You shall remember the LORD your God, for it is he who gives you power to get wealth, that he may confirm his covenant that he swore to your fathers, as it is this day."*[135]

Whether the verse was meant just for the Jews of that time as many Christians love to explain away things they do not like in the living Bible (a dodge to obedience) does not really matter, the passage in Deuteronomy gives us a glimpse of the mindset of God on the issue of wealth. It suggests that wealth is equal to good. Maybe this is how we

---

[134] Luke 6:38

[135] Deuteronomy 8:18

should read God's will for us on the subject of wealth and poverty instead of looking for a specific verse that defines everything.

However, you have to recognize the truth that if it is only God that gives us the power to make wealth. He gives to both believers and nonbelievers alike. That allows speculation and questions whether we might be praying amiss when we use prayer to ask God for wealth since He gives to both believers and nonbelievers. More specifically, if I am correct, shouldn't we be asking the question 'is praying to Jesus for personal wealth a valid and worthwhile effort?'

Please don't remind me. Yes, I am aware there are many verses in the Bible that can be used to contradict what I have just said. However, that is the nature of the beast; and you should accept it, shrug your shoulders, and keep going. It is part of God's design that some things remain a secret to humankind.

In reading the Pastor's book, there are other statements that are made that challenge the senses. For example, the Pastor says God's ultimate goal for us is character development and not comfort. He does not explain why he thinks these two goals are mutually exclusive.

In reality, God can develop your character the same way whether you live a comfortable life or live an uncomfortable one. It is the guy living a comfortable stress-free life who is best placed to help the poor, and the character of giving to the poor develops early in the rich than in a kid who grows up unsure where his next meal is going to come from. That character will tend toward self-centered driven goals. *I am hungry, I need food, I need shelter, I need clothing* will most likely be the dominant thoughts in that individual. Their view of money and wealth will always be different from the view of these same things by someone born a Rockefeller, a Ford, or lately a Walton (think Walmart). Even when a child born poor has made it, some still harbor the fear of losing it all, thereby propelling the squirrel instinct in them.

I remember reading an interview in which the late John Lennon of the Beatles said, despite his wealth, he still harbored the fear of losing it all. However, being comfortable in this life can just as easily propel one into selfless devotion to the Almighty and giving to the poor just as easily as it can lead one to Las Vegas to gamble these blessings away.

THE HOLY SPIRIT AS AN AGENT OF CHANGE

Despite the many questionable statements in this chapter, there is a lot of wisdom, useful information, and reminders in this section of his book. We are reminded for example that the process of sanctification is a long slow process that continues into the afterlife. The Holy Spirit is the agent for this transformation and that we cannot accomplish the process by our own efforts.

I like the graphic created in my mind by the fact that the Bible compares spiritual growth to a seed or a child growing up and that each metaphor requires active participation. He spoils it all though by saying the Holy Spirit operates quietly inside us. Even though I understand perfectly what he means, I am one of those Christians who sees the operation of the Holy Spirit in terms of some form of sensation when I pray as evidence of His presence in me. This might be the extreme, but once you learn to recognize that type of manifestation in you, you grow to expect it; and when it gets quiet, you worry you have offended the Almighty God.

I get more energized when I am praying for a saint and God signals His presence by manifesting in this way. It is like He is saying, "Good job, my son. Now I will take over from here." For me, this graphic for the Holy Spirit manifesting in a believer is biblical. It comes from that passage in the Bible that says, *"When the day of Pentecost came, they were all together in one place. Suddenly a sound like the blowing of a violent wind came from heaven and filled the whole house where they were sitting. They saw what seemed to be tongues of fire that separated and came to rest on each of them. All of them were filled with the Holy Spirit and began to speak in other tongues as the Spirit enabled them."*[136]

Now this happened about 2,000 years ago (1,967 to be exact) after Jesus told His disciples it would happen. If you became a believer today and soon thereafter you start to experience these same sensations, why shouldn't that be evidence that this Jesus thing is for real. In fact, in light of the lack of any physical evidence that heaven and hell exist, the Jesus thing is the only real thing we have to go by. He promised it, and it happened and is still happening.

---

[136] Acts 2:1-4

I once asked a Jewish friend out of curiosity if Holy Ghost related manifestations were common among non-Christian Jews, and she told me no. A Muslim friend also told me the same thing. Then what am I supposed to think—that I am hallucinating when I experience these things and speak in tongues? Rick Warren, being a Southern Baptist, is bound to have a different view on this subjects from what Pentecostals believe. I read the following piece recently related to Pastor Rick Warren's speech to the Assemblies of God gathering. The writer said the following:

> Speaking in tongues has arguably been the most emphasized charism of the modern Pentecostal movement. Although the leading Pentecostal denominations in the world all emphasize this gift doctrinally, some do so more than others. In fact, the largest Pentecostal organization in the world, the AG, considers tongues "the initial, physical evidence of the Baptism in the Holy Spirit." The "distinctive doctrine" of the AG is that this charism is the primary tangible evidence that a Christ-follower has experienced a "second work of grace" called the Baptism in the Holy Spirit—which believers, according to doctrinal statements, are supposed to "ardently expect" and "earnestly seek."[137]

My question to other Christians is if one's level of Christianity does not allow them to share this Pentecost experience, shouldn't that be a cause for concern? After all, Apostle Paul tells us, *"Do not get drunk on wine, which leads to debauchery. Instead, be filled with the Spirit."*[138]

MOVING AHEAD IN OUR WEAKNESS

In this chapter, we are also told that God waits for you to act first and that we should move ahead in our weakness. We often hear people say God helps those who help themselves. This is good advice because the tendency to be paralyzed when faced with a problem too big for us to

---

[137] Robert Crosby is an author and professor of Practical Theology at Southeastern University.

[138] Ephesians 5:18

handle is common. Instead of going out there and attacking the world, some of us tend to wait for the breakthrough to manifest.

However, this advice should be taken in balance with the advice not to "lean on one's own understanding." One can well ask, how are we expected to figure this out when it is something we should leave in the hands of the Almighty God and when we should "act first" so the Holy Spirit can intervene? Like most things spiritual, God leaves us to be the best judges on issues of balance. We should let our own sense of judgment reign. Knowing your Bible does come into play because that is where we get all the information that allows us to make informed judgments in all areas of our lives.

POINTS TO PONDER

What character qualities in Jesus do you admire most?

What are the things that prevent you from being like Jesus?

Have you ever gone out to preach the Good News to complete strangers?

Do you wish God had given you the gift of healing so you could heal others through prayer and to cast out demons just like Jesus did?

Do you believe that Jesus and the Apostles were a breed apart and that to be like Jesus, you would need special anointing from up above?

Do you belong to a church?

Does the Holy Spirit manifest in you when you pray?

Do you speak in tongues?

If you answered no to the last three questions, does it concern you that the Holy Spirit does not manifest in you?

Would you like the Holy Spirit to manifest in you?

Scriptures: 1 Kings 3:11-13
                Acts 2:1-4
                Ephesians 5:18

CHAPTER 22

How We Grow

(Rick Warren's Day 23)

The message in this chapter is God wants us to grow spiritually, but most Christians remain in diapers forever. Spiritual growth is the process of becoming more like Jesus. It is not automatic. We need the Holy Spirit to help us grow. Most people miss their purpose by failing to commit. To grow, God plays His part, and we play our part. A key to spiritual growth is changing the way we think.

This chapter tackles one of the most misunderstood areas in Christianity. It discusses the role of the Holy Spirit in our spiritual growth. When I first read the book, I could not quite grasp how the Holy Spirit, the spirit, and the soul interacted and what their respective functions were.

That forced me to carry out a little research of my own. I found there was a lot of literature on the subject but not much agreement. This is important for every Christian because, when the experts can't agree on the exact meaning of a Bible verse, term or word you need to pray for a revelation. This is the time to let the Holy Spirit that dwells in you guide you find the meaning that you will be comfortable with.

Remember, this is the meaning you will live with for the rest of your life because, ultimately, it is your personal walk with Jesus.

When the Pastor talks about spiritual growth the word *spiritual* quickly conjures up a series of questions.

The first one is, which spirit in involved?

What is it that grows?

Is it the spirit God breathed into Adam's nostrils at creation?

The basics are that every individual is a triune, meaning, we have a spirit, a soul, and a body. To add to the confusion, Bible verses use the word *spirit* to refer to the soul some of the time so that the two words are used interchangeably. We are also told that, when we are born again, we acquire yet another spirit, and this one is the Holy Spirit—the very same one Jesus Christ talked about nearly 2,000 years ago. So what exactly are we dealing with here?

The foundation verse says, *"Then the LORD God formed a man from the dust of the ground and breathed into his nostrils the breath of life, and the man became a living being (soul)."*[139] We can also look at the verse that says, *"May God himself, the God of peace, sanctify you through and through. May your whole spirit, soul and body be kept blameless at the coming of our Lord Jesus Christ."*[140]

The soul is who you are, your character, your individuality. Even though your individual soul did not exist before your mother and father gave life to you, it will exist forever. It cannot be killed by man.

We need to pause here and note that, since the words spirit and soul are used interchangeably in the Bible, we can never be 100 percent sure which of the two, spirit or soul, can never be killed by man. We can confirm that the spirit cannot be killed by men. The scriptures are clear on that. However, the scriptures are not so clear when it comes to the soul.

We learn from scripture above that God created man from dust. He then breathed the breath of life into His creation and the man became a living soul. For man to exist, therefore, it was necessary for the dust and God's breathe to come together for the soul to come to life. Then what happens to the soul when the body dies? Does the soul survive or it also dies leaving only the spirit?

Let us look briefly at the three parts of a human being one by one.

---

[139] Genesis 2:7

[140] 1 Thessalonian 5:23

The body—We have no problem identifying the body because it exists both in space and time. We can touch it. It is what the Apostle Paul calls the earthly tent or temporary dwelling that houses us while we are here on earth.[141] That is us in the flesh. It is also the part of us that is returned to the earth when we die.

It is a mark of how we take God for granted that we never stop to think about the complexity of this human body of ours. That even in these days of high tech, no machine has yet been created that can perform the things the human body can do without much thought. It operates through the five senses that God gave us. We have the sense of touch, sight, hearing, taste, and smell. The body uses all these senses all the time just to maintain balance.

These five senses can also get us into deep trouble with God. For example, it is through the sense of sight that we see the very things that lead to lust and eventually to temptation and sin. That tells us there is some interaction between the many parts of the body, which in turn leads us to wonder about the separate functions of the spirit, soul and body.

The Spirit—I mentioned before that God breathed into Adam's nostril the spirit that transformed him into a living soul. We all have this spirit. That means from the day we are born, we have a personal spirit in us. Otherwise, we would not have life. We have this spirit whether we are believers, nonbelievers or Satanists.

The Soul—The third part of the human being is the soul. It is sometimes referred to as the sprit as well, but the scripture suggests that it is distinct and separate. The question then becomes: What exactly is the soul? The soul comprises three parts. It is the mind, the emotions, and the will. It is said that the soul is the seat of our affections—our sense of right or wrong, of love, hate, lusts, and even the appetites of the body.

Before we can talk about spiritual growth, we need to understand the different functions of the spirit and the soul. Literally speaking, the function of the spirit is to contact God, and we do that through worship. The Bible tells us that *"God is Spirit, and those who worship Him must worship in spirit and truthfulness."*[142] We are also told that God

---

[141] 1 Corinthian 5:1
[142] John 4.24

made the spirit for the purpose of dwelling in us,[143] and the Apostle Paul tells us the spirit of man knows his thoughts, which suggests that our thoughts originate in either the soul or the body and not in our personal spirit.[144] Each of these passages reveals something about the spirit and its functions.

The other two functions of the spirit are to receive God and to contain God. We received this spirit, better known as the Holy Spirit, when we were born again. The Holy Spirit displaces the spirit of the world in us and actually resides in our personal spirit, only if we permit this to happen by accepting the authority of the Bible and living by it.

We contain God when the Holly Spirit resides in our personal spirit.

The situation gets a little more complicated when one reads in 1 John 4:1 that we should not believe every spirit, but we should test the spirit to make sure it is from God. This passage suggests that there are other spirits that can dwell within us, but clearly, they do not have the same functions as our personal spirit. As we continue to study the Bible, we discover that there is the spirit of the world and the spirit of God (Holy Spirit), both of which can influence our personal spirit. From the time we are born, we are exposed to the spirit of the world. It influences us as we develop our basic character and worldly habits. When we repent and come to Jesus Christ, the Holy Spirit displaces this spirit of the world.

We know that only God gives life. Then how does the spirit of the world get involved? The devil can corrupt our personal spirit, but only after it has come into the human child when it is born. It seems that for believers, our personal spirit has confessed Jesus because Galatians 6:18 tells us that the grace of the Lord Jesus will be with us if we so confess.

Nonbelievers, on the other hand, have not confessed Jesus, and the spirit of the world remains dominant in their lives. They live life as they feel. This statement can provoke others like Muslims and, to a certain extent, the Jews who, while they worship the same God as Christians, explicitly deny that Jesus was the Messiah, the Son of God.

It is not easy to distinguish between the spirit and the soul. A body without a spirit is a dead body, but when the spirit and the body were combined in Adam, he became a living soul. The spirit thus activates the soul, which is that part of us that gives us our character or personality.

---

[143] James 4:5

[144] 1 Corinthian 2:11

The question of course is whether what God breathed into Adam to give him life was the spirit the Pastor is referring to when he discusses spiritual growth. The answer is of course not. When you become born again, you receive the Holy Spirit, which resides in you but is not part of you. It resides in your spirit as opposed to your soul and from that location seeks to influence your soul, character, and behavior. It is able to shape your soul and character or personality to make you Christlike. In other words, while only born-again Christians have the Holy Spirit residing in them, every member of the human race also has a body, a spirit and a soul.

The Pastor explains that, when you convert to Christianity, only your personal spirit is involved. Yes, you become saved for Jesus's Kingdom, but your old habits are still the same. It is these old habits that need to change if a new creation that is obedient to God is to emerge. This is a process that the Pastor calls spiritual growth. It is the process by which one is transformed from being a sinner before they are born again to the new Christlike person that emerges.

He says if you are an alcoholic, the process of becoming a sober you begins when you convert. This change does not happen overnight but can take from a few days to several years to complete, depending. If one is a drug addict, the process of recovering is part of this transformation from within. It follows that if one is born again but does nothing to turn away from these old ways, there is no spiritual growth there.

The scary part of all this according to the Pastor is that it seems to mirror the situation many Christians find themselves in our day and age. Pastor Warren makes the statement that "sadly, millions of Christians grow older but never grow up spiritually." He says they have accepted Jesus, but nothing else about them has changed. That means if they were prostitutes, adulterers, or fornicators, thieves, murders, etc., that lifestyle continues even as they continue to go to church every Sunday and to do all the things expected of a true believer.

It is unfortunate that the Pastor given his insightful approach stopped short of getting into the practical aspects of this teaching. What is the status of this person who has accepted Jesus but is unable or is incapable of following God's precepts? If the teaching by mainline Evangelicals is "once saved always saved," how do we reconcile this with the situation of a believer who continues to sin? Apostle Paul's admonition that once you accepted Jesus, you cannot continue to sin seems unequivocal. I have asked this question elsewhere in this book and tried to answer it.

Growing up in an African Christian family, I saw firsthand what can happen. It was accepted that one can be both a Christian and an adulterer. In a culture that permits polygamy, issues of fornication and adultery are not that easy to deal with. There was no bar against fornication among the young, and as is also true for most Western Christian cultures, including the British and American cultures. Sex before marriage is condoned, if not by the church, definitely by society.

Surprisingly, we find stricter adherence to the "No sex before marriage" teaching in Muslim cultures. Why is that? Is it possible that by preaching the "once saved always saved" doctrine, we encourage this behavior?

In the culture I grew up in, it was not unusual for a Christian father to stop by the bar on his way back from church and get wasted. The whole concept of Christianity as a way of life did not quite exist except for the very few. Some church people did not see anything wrong with consulting spiritual mediums whenever they felt a need to do so. That is worshipping other Gods, and the Christian God is a jealous God[145] who will not accept that.

POINTS TO PONDER

What is spiritual growth?
What is the spirit of the world?
How does it influence our habits?
What is the role of the soul?
What is the role of the spirit?
What is the role of the Holy Spirit?
What replaces the spirit of the world as we grow spiritually?
If the soul is the result of God's breath and dust, what happens to the soul at death?

Scriptures: 1 Thessalonians 5:23
             Genesis 2:7

---

[145] Exodus 20:4-6

CHAPTER 23

Transformed by Trouble

(Warren's Day 25)

We will learn that God has a purpose behind every problem. We are reminded that God could have kept Joseph out of jail, Daniel out of the lion's den, and the three Hebrew boys out of the blazing furnace; but He didn't because that was His purpose. None of our problems could happen without God's permission. We are forced to Jesus by trouble.

Pastor Warren preaches to the converted when he says trouble pushes us closer to God. One thing I have learned in life is that people seek God when things are not going great in their lives. A guy who has a great job, a great marriage, and a happy home is not looking for many answers from God. If he is a believer, he will thank God every day of his life for God's blessings. I am sure the Hollywood crowd would be in this category if Satan had not perfected his number one attack weapon, especially for the young and rich—fornication and infidelity in marriage.

On the other hand, a guy in the trenches who needs a breakthrough in business, at home, at work, or in his marriage has more reason to seek God. It follows that circumstances have an influence on worship. If you're a parent, there is nothing that will drive you to Jesus faster than a child getting into an accident or becoming seriously ill.

The same goes for a breadwinner who suddenly finds himself on the unemployment line with all those mouths to feed back home. In short, when things stop going right, people tend to look to a higher authority for divine intervention.

The only issue to emerge from my reading of this chapter is the idea that all bad things that happen to people, happen with God's permission. This proposition clearly has its roots in what happened with Job in the Bible.

In Job, we learn that *"one day the angels came to present themselves before the* LORD, *and Satan also came with them. The* LORD *said to Satan, 'Where have you come from?' Satan answered the* LORD, *'From roaming throughout the earth, going back and forth on it.' Then the* LORD *said to Satan, 'Have you considered my servant Job? There is no one on earth like him; he is blameless and upright, a man who fears God and shuns evil.' 'Does Job fear God for nothing?' Satan replied. 'Have you not put a hedge around him and his household and everything he has? You have blessed the work of his hands, so that his flocks and herds are spread throughout the land. But now stretch out your hand and strike everything he has, and he will surely curse you to your face.' The* LORD *said to Satan, 'Very well, then, everything he has is in your power, but on the man himself do not lay a finger.' Then Satan went out from the presence of the* LORD."[146]

This passage informed us of the relationship between God and Lucifer. It is clear that Satan was still a member of God's inner circle, although clearly the black sheep of the family. The view that God allows all bad things to happen is based on disputed interpretations of the scriptures. There is an equally plausible view in Christianity that a combination of our free will and the works of the devil can cause us trouble. A murderous thief has free will to come into your home intending to steal but could end up killing someone. The devil is the primary player in the life of the thief and everything he does. What and where did God enter the picture in this situation?

Pastor Warren on page 195 returns to his theme of predestination when he writes, "Because every day of your life was written on God's calendar before you were born, everything that happens to you has spiritual significance." He then gives us his take on the verse that says, *"And we know that all things work together for good to them that love God,*

---

[146] Job 1:6-12

to them who are the called according to his purpose."[147] Others interpret this verse to mean that if you trust in the Lord, a mix of good and bad things all work for the good in the end. The Pastor, on the other hand, says the verse does not mean there will be a happy ending. All this can be confusing.

It also means conclusions reached by stringing together disputed dogma in the Christian church are not necessarily valid.

We know, on the one hand, that Satan represents an ever present menace to believers as he tries to get them to disobey God. Our best guide to knowing how the devil operates is Ephesians 6. I take it that the message the Apostle Paul wanted to convey was we should always keep on the full armor of God to defend against any satanic attacks. Fair enough, but it creates an apparent contradiction when we learn from Job that Satan operates under license from God. In other words, Satan cannot attack us unless God approves. If one has on the full armor of God, why should Satan be able to attack the believer's fortified defenses unless an element of unconfessed sin is involved?

The question then becomes: Why would God allow satanic attacks on His own believers? There has to be a trigger that causes God to do this, no? In Job, no reason is given other than God deciding to allow the devil to test Job to prove a point. The message in Job is thus very difficult to swallow for many Christians because this was a righteous man who always did the right thing. Then why would God give Satan permission to literally decimate Job the way he did? This remains one of those questions that have never been completely answered by the scriptures.

For today's Christian, the question is does Satan continue to enjoy the same access to God as he did in Job's time even after Jesus brought us the new covenant. The answer to this question is yes and no. There is no one scripture that clarifies the issue. The Gospel of John gives us what maybe the best answer. It suggests that the relationship between God and Satan underwent a change of sorts, even though we are left unsure what exactly. The two verses say, *"Now is the judgment of this world. Now shall the prince of this world be cast out. And I, if I am lifted up from the earth, I will draw all to Myself."*[148]

---

[147] Romans 8:28-29

[148] John 12:31-32

It would seem that, when Jesus ascended to heaven, Satan was finally expelled from heaven. We also learn from Revelation that "the great dragon was hurled down—that ancient serpent called the devil, or Satan, who leads the whole world astray. He was hurled to the earth, and his angels with him. Then I heard a loud voice in heaven say: *"Now have come the salvation and the power and the kingdom of our God, and the authority of his Messiah. For the accuser of our brothers and sisters, who accuses them before our God day and night, has been hurled down. They triumphed over him by the blood of the Lamb and by the word of their testimony; they did not love their lives so much as to shrink from death. Therefore rejoice, you heavens and you who dwell in them! But woe to the earth and the sea, because the devil has gone down to you! He is filled with fury, because he knows that his time is short."*[149]

The verse 12 of the above scripture shows clearly that Satan is here on earth, full of fury and trying his best to tempt us into sin. Apostle Paul in Ephesian 6 tells us how the devil goes about doing this. It seems that our own sin nature and actual sin open us to the attacks by the devil. Pastor Warren has devoted two chapters to this subject, and I personally found them very helpful in my efforts to understand temptation—Satan and his method of attack. I find the chapters have left me better able to resist temptation.

This brings us to the issue also discussed by the Pastor why God tests us with trials and tribulations in the first place. Pastor Warren's statement that God tests us as part of his plan to develop character is biblical, and he quotes a number of scriptures to support his statement. Left unresolved, however, is how we distinguish between problems that are God induced and those that are the result of satanic attacks.

Furthermore, at some point the question has to be asked whether these concepts about God deliberately introducing problems into our lives to test us are not a violation of our own view of God's character. Remember, all good things come from God!

I accept the proposition that God can punish, but He punishes for a reason. The devil, on the other hand, is a counterforce that stands in opposition to everything God does or to His will for us. My human view of the situation is that the devil attacks believers, and God comes to the rescue. There are many scriptures that suggest this, and Psalm 91 is

---

[149] Revelation 12:9-12

just but one of them. The following verses in that Psalm are particularly instructive when they say, *"'Because he loves me,' says the* LORD, *'I will rescue him; I will protect him, for he acknowledges my name. He will call on me, and I will answer him; I will be with him in trouble, I will deliver him and honor him. With long life I will satisfy him and show him my salvation.'"*[150] The two preceding verses tell us that God *"will command his angels concerning you (us) to guard you (us) in all your (our) ways; they will lift you(us) up in their hands, so that you (we) will not strike your foot against a stone."*[151].

These verses seem to reflect a situation where, if we are in trouble, (attacked) we can call on Him to come to our rescue once the attack has already happened, and He will come. This last idea suggests that, when attacked, God is unaware of Satan's attack. This is a common experience in our churches. There is an accident that threatens life, and we all join in prayer to reverse the situation. God comes to the rescue, and what could have required a serious surgical operation is diffused to the surprise of even the doctors who were already planning to operate.

These theories of course challenge concepts concerning God's foreknowledge. If we accept that God indeed has foreknowledge of everything, these theories just add to our confusion.

This is not to deny the evidence of God's wrath. The Old Testament is replete with examples of God punishing the Jews for various acts of disobedience and unbelief. We are punished for our disobedience here on earth and also in hell, if one happens to end up there. In truth, given that the God we worship is a forgiving God, the question on why He would allow a fatal accident to happen to the child of a believer remains unanswered.

While Christians will accept what the Pastor has to say on this issue as dogma, there are lingering questions on why a forgiving God would allow these attacks to happen in the first place. The Pastor makes statements that God is in complete control of every situation while accepting at the same time that Satan operates in our lives in direct opposition to God's intentions for us. There has to be something that forces God to accept the continued existence of the devil or allow the devil to attack believers.

---

[150] Psalm 91:13-14

[151] Psalm 91:11-12

Everything points to a possible covenant between God and Lucifer that gave the latter certain legal rights here on earth. Christians appear unable to explain this in clear enough terms for all of us to understand. If indeed Satan has legal rights, it will be because God has allowed that situation to exist. We try to make sense of this without much success, which in turn leads to wild theories about the relationship between God and Satan.

I once read a passage from a nonreligious source, which means it is an unreliable source for our purposes here, that suggested that God (Jesus) and Satan were like brothers fighting over an inheritance that they received from their father (God the Father). I also understand that the Mormons actually preach this doctrine.

Why do we have such wild theories about such a thing?

The reason is we try to make sense of His ways and His thoughts using our own human understanding that says if X is equal to Y and Y is equal to Z, then Z is equal to X. However, that is human logic, not God's way of thinking.

That God is a mystery should be understood and accepted by all. He says, *"For my thoughts are not your thoughts, neither are your ways my ways."*[152] Even though the context of that quotation was His pardoning nature and disposition, the passage offers us clear guidance on this issue. There has to be a lot we do not know about God to explain some of these things that remain a mystery.

It remains true that God controls everything, but when bad things happen, we are entitled to ask why if God controls everything did He allow something like this to happen.

In my traditional African belief system, people worshipped the dead because they regarded their dead ancestors as spirit guardians with a duty to protect those they left behind at death. When bad things happen, people made the logical assumption that this happened because they had done something to anger their spirit guardians. Hence, the necessity to atone for whatever one had done to anger ancestral spirits.

Notice how close this belief system is to the Old Testament idea of offering a sacrifice to atone for our sins. That system of course died with Christ for Christians.

---

[152]   Isaiah 55:8

The idea that, when you sin, God turns away from you is common to many belief systems. The Bible uses the word *quench* to explain how the Holy Spirit, while continuing to indwell you the believer, can stop doing some things He does that are beneficial to your spiritual growth.

Finally, we need to look at what happens when someone has an accident. Those who argue that God controls everything have to consider situations where God allows a child to be in an accident, but then quickly answers our prayers and the doctors save the life.

What is the dynamic at work here that would cause God to allow the accident to happen because the devil has asked for permission but just as quickly change His mind and allow the doctors to save the victim? The experience has all the hallmarks of a sneak attack. A better view in my mind is to say, while God's attention is distracted elsewhere, Satan can operate to our detriment, but that our prayers quickly draw God's attention to the tragedy and hopefully to a healing. That sounds like what Psalms 91 is about, but that is just my human logic working here.

POINTS TO PONDER

What brought you to Jesus Christ?

Do you believe in predestination?

Do you believe Satan attacks us because of our sins?

Do you think confessing our sins daily keeps the devil from attacking us?

If you do, how do you explain children who are born with serious defects?

Do you blame God?

Do you blame Satan?

Scriptures: John 12:31-32
                Revelation 12:9-12
                Psalm 91:11-12; 14-19

CHAPTER 24

(Warren's Day 26-28)

-GROWING THROUGH TEMPTATION-
-DEFEATING TEMPTATION-
-IT TAKES TIME-

We will learn in these three chapters that every temptation is an opportunity to do good. We are told about the nine character qualities of Jesus and that God allows us to develop these qualities in our lives by allowing circumstances in which we are tempted to do the exact opposite. We are told how temptation works and how to overcome it. In chapter 27, we are given strategies for defeating temptation; and in chapter 29, we are told all this takes time.

I found these three chapters to be very useful and very enlightening indeed, and for me, they are part of the reason his book became a bestseller. They gave me new insights into the issue of temptation, defeating it and resisting it. We learn along the way that there are no shortcuts to spiritual growth and that it takes a lifetime and that the process continues into the afterlife.

We learn some strategies for resisting temptation, and one of my favorites is the Pastor's advice to take note of who is there when we are most tempted. Clearly, the trick works well in connection with sexual immorality. If you know there is sexual tension between you and a member of the opposite sex, and you want to avoid temptation, you make sure you are never alone with that person. You act the opposite of what you would do if you were pursuing that person for a romantic relationship. Instead of dinner for two, make it dinner for three or more.

The message is very clear, and this is the type of advice one can apply to all areas of one's life where one faces challenges with sin. If you have a tendency for excessive drinking, avoid nightclubs and places that tend to make you drink to excess.

The issue of temptation and sin has always been a source of confusion for me, as it probably is for many other Christians. One has to agree that Pastor Rick Warren has done a marvelous job of making us understand. The idea that every temptation is an opportunity to do good is a very enlightening idea indeed in as far as it leads us to look at an everyday issue from a completely different perspective. That mindset makes it easy to modify our reaction to situations that can lead us to do evil.

Looking at the character of Jesus in terms of the fruit of the spirit makes Him understandable to us as well. The Pastor quotes the Bible when he says, *"When the Holy Spirit controls our lives, he will produce this kind of fruit in us: love, joy, peace, patience, kindness, goodness, fruitfulness, gentleness, and self-control."*[153] This brings Jesus to life in our minds. The Pastor says God develops the fruit of the spirit in our lives by allowing us to experience circumstances in which we are tempted to express the exact opposite quality.

It should not escape the believer that love, joy, and peace are enjoyed in community with others; and to enjoy them, you need to surround yourself with the right types of people. Love, joy, and peace are not possible in a marriage where fidelity is not respected by either partner. When one party to the marriage is involved in adultery, unless the innocent party is completely unaware of it, the quality of life for the innocent spouse and the children, if children are involved, is adversely affected.

---

[153] Galatians 6:1-2

The self-centeredness of people involved in adultery is clear and obvious. Experience, therefore, shows that one or both partners in a marriage can contribute to the lack of joy and peace in the home by their infidelity. There is always an aggressive partner who provokes the situation, and if I were counseling the couple, I would focus on the aggressor. In Family Courts in America, the aggressive partner, especially if a woman, gets support from the courts because their focus is not love, peace, and joy; but simply preventing the violence in the home that normally accompanies strife and infidelity.

That many marriages could be served if these courts were expanded to include a marriage counseling service as a first step before a case gets before the judge is an amazing omission, especially given the expenses broken marriages bring on the state governments.

I also found the section on how temptation works very helpful as well. The devil feasts on our normal desires. This establishes the fact that temptation starts from within us. For example, both men and women have sexual needs, and where they are unfulfilled, people find other ways of meeting these needs. The God ordained way of doing this is with your spouse. Knowing this, Christians and non-Christians alike have to navigate this obstacle course that is marriage with care, that is, if the marriage is to remain intact.

It is noteworthy in this connection that both the Lord Jesus Christ and Apostle Paul were unmarried. They did this to better devote their lives to their calling—their work for the Kingdom of God. The sacrifices of preaching the Gospel were in their view incompatible with having a wife and kids to deal with. That tells us that God realizes that marriage imposes certain challenges on the individual, certain responsibilities unique to that situation, including the raising of children.

Jesus clearly stated His preference and its justification. Yet in some Christian literature, people suggest that Jesus supported the idea that people should not marry. That is a clear misunderstanding of that scripture. In the Gospel of Matthew, Jesus did not suggest that people should remain unmarried but expressed a preference for that state for people involved with spreading the Good News. He was teaching on celibacy, and I will let that passage (NIV) speak for itself. It says, *"His disciples said to Him, 'If such is the case of the man with his wife, it is better not to marry.' But He said to them, 'All cannot accept this saying, but only those to whom it has been given: For there are eunuchs who were born thus from their mother's womb, and there are eunuchs who were made eunuchs by men, and there are eunuchs who have made themselves eunuchs for the kingdom of heaven's sake. He who is able to accept it, let him accept it.'"*[154]

We have to be mindful that all the disciples were married men and a command from Jesus for people not to marry would have meant an end to procreation as we know it. Jesus never intended that.

In that same passage, another error of Christian dogma is exposed. Jesus was careful to point out that not everybody can accept the idea that people should not marry, "but only those to whom it has been given." There is a tendency in Christian literature to assume that everything in the Bible is applicable to all Christians, even when it was said to a king or a prophet under special circumstances.

We are also told in this chapter that doubt, deception, and disobedience are the other steps the devil uses in order for us to consummate the sin. In other words, the process of temptation involves the three steps: identifying a desire in us, introducing doubt in us, and then deception. If the tempted falls for this, sin is committed, and Satan wins.

For me, though, this whole issue of temptation and sin and the unlimited pardons (God's mercy) that are involved create confusion among Christians. Logically, though the premise that "once saved always saved" is not settled dogma in Christian literature. This is because there is so much scripture on both sides of the debate. The Lord Jesus says, *"And so I tell you, every kind of sin and slander can be forgiven, but blasphemy against the Spirit will not be forgiven. Anyone who speaks a word against the Son of Man will be forgiven, but anyone who speaks against the Holy Spirit will not be forgiven, either in this age or in the age to come."*[155]

We learn from this that all sins except one will be forgiven. The other scriptures are clear that we need to repent in order to be forgiven. The present debate is about automatic forgiveness once you have accepted Christ. When we convert to Christianity and confess that Jesus is Lord over our lives, it is said that we are forgiven all our past, present, and future sins. According to some leading theologians, we do not need to ask God for forgiveness ever again.

---

[154] Matthew 19:10-12

[155] Matthew 12:32

However, that position runs counter to the Lord's Prayer that has us asking for forgiveness every day, so the question becomes why then do we need to confess our sins every day.

I remember listening to a clip on YouTube by Dr. Charles Stanley of In Touch Ministry in which he explains all this. He says we have a relationship with God which starts with what the Apostle John tells us, *"If we confess our sins, he is faithful and just and will forgive us our sins and purify us from all unrighteousness."*[156] In our daily walk with God, sin has the effect of interfering with our fellowship with God. Therefore, when we confess and ask for forgiveness of our sins, we are only doing that to restore our fellowship with God.

Under normal circumstances, that explanation should take care of the fact that we have been taught since childhood to ask God on a daily basis to forgive us our trespasses as we forgive those who have trespassed against us. Others argue that if God forgives believers all their sins automatically, what is there to stop us from continuing to sin when it suits our purposes and coming forward and confessing our sins to restore our fellowship with God? This argument is part of the "once saved, always saved" doctrine.

Others reject that doctrine and claim the idea is a lie and quote Apostle Paul to support their argument. The Apostle asks and answers his own question. He says, *"What shall we say, then? Shall we go on sinning so that grace may increase?"*[157] He answers his own question by saying, "By no means! We died to sin; how can we live in it any longer?"

This answer should satisfy the opponents of the "once saved, always saved" school of thought and set us straight on the issue, but it fails to answer the follow-up question which is: If we continue to sin, what happens then? Doesn't there come a time when God says enough is enough and stops hearing us?

The scripture that says, *"If we deliberately keep on sinning after we have received the knowledge of the truth, no sacrifice for sins is left, but only a fearful expectation of judgment and of raging fire that will consume the enemies of God,"*[158] seems to support that view.

---

[156] John 1:9

[157] Romans 6:1-2

[158] Hebrews 10:26-27

Should we, therefore, conclude that there is a limit to God's forgiveness for those who continue to sin? This conclusion seems logical if we assume that we have a full understanding of what being saved is. It clearly contradicts the whole "once saved, always saved" school of thought and those Bible verses that hold that God will always forgive.

Either way, we take this a debate—there are no winners. The bottom line is, if you have the Holy Spirit dwelling in you, you cannot continue sinning and then look for an escape hatch by interpreting the Bible to cover up for your sinning.

Yet Jesus's own words in Matthew above add to the confusion by telling us every sin except blasphemy against the Holy Spirit will be forgiven. He does not address the question of repeated (or continual) sin.

Under the Old Testament, we know that the rules were different. In Numbers, we learn that anyone who sins defiantly blasphemed the Lord, and such a person was to be cut off from his people.[159] That was a sin unto death, one presumes that Apostle John is talking about when he says, *"If you see any brother or sister commit a sin that does not lead to death, you should pray and God will give them life. I refer to those whose sin does not lead to death. There is a sin that leads to death. I am not saying that you should pray about that. All wrongdoing is sin, and there is sin that does not lead to death."*[160]

The real point of this scripture is that we, as Christians, can intercede for a brother or sister who is committing a less serious sin, and God will forgive that sinner. For more serious sins, we do not have this authority. The sinner himself/herself has to repent and ask for forgiveness. Apostle John, however, omitted to identify the sins that lead unto death and those that do not, and in so doing has ignited a debate that continues to rage. The question is: What did he mean by this scripture? There is not even agreement as to whether the death here is physical death or spiritual death.

Others have looked to the Old Testament for a possible answer. They argue that sins that were considered serious and whose commission led to serious consequences are what the Apostle had in mind. That means that sins involving sexual immorality would be considered sins unto death. The list includes fornicators, idolaters, adulterers, and effeminate abusers

---

[159] Numbers 15:30
[160] 1 John 5:16-17

of themselves with mankind, thieves, covetous, drunkards, revilers, and extortionist.[161]

The good news is this does not mean people who commit these sins will not be forgiven, but that a brother/sister cannot intercede for them and ask God to forgive them. They have to do that themselves. Then this does not contradict Jesus's statement that all sins can be forgiven except blasphemy.

The Pastor ends this part of his helpful book with some reassuring words about the time element (page 217) involved in spiritual growth. He says it takes time to develop a Christlike character.

The war analogy he uses is also very useful. He says the moment we open ourselves to Jesus, God gets a "beachhead" into our lives. Then the hard work of conquering all areas of our sinning lives begins. He says Christlikeness is your destination, but your journey will last a lifetime. To answer the question on why does it take so long, he answers that bad habits take a lifetime to develop. Therefore, it makes sense that it should take a long time to undo them.

One also has to look at the challenges people face in life while they are trying to grow spiritually. Personal circumstances can play a role in the process of breaking bad habits. For example, the Bible advises everyone to get a wife or husband to avoid sexual immorality. For a mother of two trying to find Mr. Right, this can be a vexing undertaking.

In today's world where men play games and avoid commitment, one can just imagine the lifestyle of a Christian woman in her late thirties or early forties trying to find that Mr. Right. How long can you date in a world of unbelievers and avoid sex before marriage? Some people in this situation find themselves having to compromise their personal moral standards in order to be accepted despite the extra baggage (children) they bring into the new relationship. Many men have no problems with these situations as long as they get all the sex they want, but when the topic of marriage starts to heat up, they move on.

As a result, this process becomes a trial-and-error-type situation with each failed relationship representing a step backwards in terms of one's spiritual growth. It is two steps up the ladder, and one step backwards.

I know of one situation of a woman who came to church regularly but stopped coming each time she got involved sexually with a new man. She

---

[161] I Corinthian 6:9-10

thought it would be hypocritical for her to come to church while living in sin. Fornication becomes very much a part of the existence of these people. There is an ever-present temptation for people in this situation. They give in because they are hoping that this will make the new man stay. They figure they will right all this with God by marrying the man.

Now before some of you remind me that the scriptures encourage self-control, let me just say self-control in the world we live in is not the easiest of options. Marriage is of course a two-way street, and it can only happen when the two lovers agree.

Before you remind me again about God's position on divorce, let me confess that I am just as confused about that subject as the next guy. In a world where some leading pastors are divorcees, not many people can give a satisfactory answer. However, once divorce has occurred, one tries to cope as best as they can and hope God will forgive whatever sin is involved.

Pastors are duty bound to offer only the self-control option, but reality is a daunting obstacle to self-control in the world we live in. A good example is a man already paying two ex-wives child support and is now considering a third try at marriage. Having failed twice, he is very aware of the odds he will fail again. A third child support possibility might keep him wary of another commitment, yet his physical needs force him into an immoral relationship with a woman.

In a culture where unbelievers outnumber believers (68:32), this is a real problem and is very evident in many churches. The real question is, if these people are saved except for their daily walk with Christ, does daily confession really restore their fellowship with God even as they continue to fornicate?

POINTS TO PONDER

What strategies do you use to avoid temptation?
Do you agree that every temptation is an opportunity to do good?
Can you explain your answer?
Once under the cross, can we continue to sin?
Is there a limit to sinning for those under the cross?

Scriptures: John 1:9
             Matthew 12:32
             1 John 5:16-17

EPILOGUE

Dedication to Zikhayi Mucheto Sithole

I recently lost an uncle who was a rare Christian in my family. He was a rare Christian because, to all intents and purposes, once he converted to Christianity, he never looked back. However, unlike his cousins who were also Christians, he turned his lifestyle into a Christian lifestyle. The occult and other heathen practices were all things of the past for him.

In 2002, it was revealed to our extended family that for more than a century and half, the family had survived and multiplied under a covenant with King Soshangane's spirit medium. King Soshangane was the Nguni King who founded the Gaza Empire, an empire that covered much of Mozambique and Eastern Zimbabwe. He ruled from 1820 to 1858. The covenant my ancestor entered into broke a curse of death that had plagued the family during the early to mid-nineteenth century. The curse had killed everyone in our family except for just two people, a brother and his sister.

According to the oral history of the family, my great-grandfather, Ndabatapashi Kuthiya Mucheto, and his sister were the only survivors of that curse. The story goes that my great-grandfather, who must have been a teen at that point, met the king's spirit medium, a man by the name of Chimoto, who saw in my ancestor a deep sorrow and inquired of him. My ancestor told the medium about the curse.

My ancestor's story must have troubled the king's spirit medium enough to cause him to seek out my great-grandfather a few weeks later and offer him help. The help came in the form of a covenant that broke the curse. Instead of dying, my ancestor married a total of four wives and had children from all four. The evidence of the covenant entered into was the paraphernalia associated with the covenant that was finally surrendered back to the successors of the king and his spirit medium in 2002.

WHAT CAUSED THE CURSE OF DEATH

Throughout the tales concerning this curse, we are never told what brought about the curse that almost erased our bloodline. Two stories are often whispered in family circles.

THE PREGNANT GIRL

A story has long circulated about a young woman who was impregnated by one of my ancestors. In line with local culture, she fled her father's home for my ancestor's as was the custom. If a girl became pregnant, she was sent to the home of the man responsible for the pregnancy. Our ancestors rejected her and sent her back to her family. Unfortunately, she never made it back. She was attacked and killed by a lion. Her family, in anger, are believed to have retaliated with the curse.

MY ANCESTOR, THE HUNTER

The second story says that one of my ancestors was a hunter. The problem was, whenever he went hunting with others and encountered game, the others would see lions instead and run away, leaving him to make the kill. Thus, while other men returned home empty handed from these hunting trips, my ancestor always came home with meat for his family.

That led the others to accuse him of using magic during these hunts, an allegation he of course denied. Eventually, my ancestor went to the chief asking for an apology and demanding damages from those who falsely accused him. He won his case, but nothing was ever paid out to him. He demanded that the chief make sure he was paid, but when the chief ignored his demands, he burnt down the chief's village. In the oral history of the family, that chief is identified as chief Musikavanhu, a dynasty that still reigns today. Though it is never mentioned, it is possible some people died in that fire.

Either one of these two acts by one of my ancestors would justify a curse of death on the family. Clearly, it was not this ancestor of mine who committed these acts, for he was himself a victim of the curse. It has to be his father or someone else from an earlier generation who committed these acts.

At any rate, nobody in our family knows the exact cause of the curse or which ancestor was responsible. A curse, however, by its nature, affects the whole bloodline.

By the same token, nobody knows for sure what my great-grandfather Kuthiya gave up in order to save his bloodline. All we know is whatever was done worked. His life changed. He married four wives, one after another. Each of the wives bore him two children, a boy and a girl. That pattern, a limit of two children from each wife and the fact each of those first three wives bore him a boy and a girl, convinced everyone that they were dealing with a supernatural event.

DATING THE COVENANT

While it is difficult to date the covenant, it is probable that this happened during King Mzila's reign (1864-1884). Mzila was the son of King Soshangane and heir to the Nguni throne of the Gaza Empire. Mzila was succeeded by his son, King Ngungunyane, who ruled until 1895 when he was arrested by the Portuguese and exiled, first to Lisbon, Portugal, and later to the Azores Islands where he died in 1906.

That was also the year my father Mutini Shadreck Nhliziyo was born. He was the first child of my grandfather, Hlebayi Batwini Nhliziyo, and using a twenty-year generational gap between father and son, my grandfather must have been born sometime in the 1880s.

It is difficult to date my great-grandfather's date of birth because of his four wives, and the fact that each marriage might have occurred several years after the previous one. For example, my grandfather was from my ancestor's third wife, and there is no telling how many years elapsed before my great-grandfather took the second and then the third wife.

For example, I believe that my father, who was born in 1906, was only a few years younger than his uncle, Chaita, the son from his grandfather's fourth wife, and there was a gap of some nineteen years between my father and his cousin, Zikhayi Sithole. Therefore, it is entirely possible that my great-grandfather was born before the 1860s. That would mean he was most likely born during Soshangane's reign (1820-1956). The most likely date for the covenant that broke the curse of death on our family must have occurred sometime during King Mzila's reign (1864-1884) but it could have happened much earlier. We know the family had started to multiply by the 1880s because that is about the time Kuthiya took a third wife. My grandfather, Hlebayi, must have been born around that time.

MY NDAU/NGUNI LINEAGE

A complicating issue in our history is we are not sure whether Kuthiya was himself Nguni or Ndau, one of the tribes conquered by the Ngunis in the eastern part of Zimbabwe. Two of his three names, Ndabatapashi and Mucheto, are definitely Ndau. The chief whose village one of my ancestors burned down was Musikavanhu, also a Ndau.

There is also speculation that one of those three names might have been the name of Kuthiya's father. Furthermore, unless the name Ndabatapashi and Mucheto were nicknames, it would appear that this man was a Ndau who married at least two Nguni women. One theory has it that Mucheto (the edge of the field) was a nickname given by reason of the many deaths in the family. People were buried at the edge of the field in those days.

Ndabatapashi, which means to hold or to touch the ground, is said to have come from the fact that the Nguni kings when they traveled up and down their empire would leave certain people in charge of an area in their absence. Hence, the theory is that having married a Nguni, that is if he wasn't one himself, he must have been one of these assimilated overseers delegated some responsibilities over an area while the king and his immediate entourage were away.

It is known that the Nguni chiefs encouraged intermarriage with the tribes they conquered as a way of consolidating power and control in these areas. They also had a policy of assimilating the local chiefs and their henchmen into their ranks, sometimes through marriage. It is possible that Ndabatapashi, a local Ndau man, married one of the Nguni ladies because the sons from his second and third wives had Nguni names.

My grandfather's two names, Hlebani and Batwini, are both Nguni names. He, in turn, also married a Nguni woman. This part of the story I know firsthand from my own great-grandmother on my father's mother's side. She was pure Nguni. This frail old lady liked to recount to us stories about our history. She also told us the story of the forced relocation of the Ngunis from the Checheche area of Mozambique, where they had settled to Biyeni in Southern Mozambique in 1889.

She made the track to Biyeni with at least two of her older daughters. Her other two daughters were much younger than the first two, suggesting they might have been born after the Biyeni sojourn. These two were only slightly older than my father who was born in 1906.

According to her account of that forced relocation, people traveled in a convoy for days on end, and those who were too weak to keep pace were left by the wayside to die. It was clear that the trip to Biyeni involved the Nguni king and his immediate family and some of his fighters and their families as well. It was as though they were being exiled to Biyeni by the Portuguese authorities who ruled the area at that time.

The forced move to Biyeni was part of the Portuguese many attempts to contain a recalcitrant King Ngungunyane.

There is nothing that suggests that my grandfather, Batwini Hlebani Nhliziyo, was part of that track to Biyeni, which suggests that the family he married into must have returned to the area sometime before 1906. My grandfather was the only one of the four half brothers who converted to Christianity. I never met him. He died before I was born. I, however, grew up around his sister, Potapi Charekwa, and her family.

My uncle Zikhayi's father was Chaita Mucheto Sithole and was the son of my great-grandfather's fourth and last wife. Chaita also had a sibling, a sister.

EVIDENCE OF THE COVENANT

The Nguni paraphernalia associated with the covenant remained in the family for more than a century and a half. By all accounts, the children of Kuthiya's first wife and their descendants were the custodians of the covenant and the related paraphernalia. The custodian was also responsible for carrying out the annual rituals required to maintain the covenant. The covenant and the related paraphernalia passed from one member of that family to the next at death.

Kuthiya had the following sons from his four wives:

1. Mafofo (His sister was Mwarira)
2. Unzwana (His sister was Mugweye)
3. Hlebani (His sister was Potapi)
4. Chaita (His sister was Ruvimbo)

The first son born to Kuthiya was Mafofo. Kuthiya's sons had the following children:

MAFOFO	UNZWANA	HLEBAYI	CHAITA
Ruben	Muhlako	Mutini	Saizi
Zaba Jangwa	Masvongwa	Ndambi	Zikhayi
Zikhuyumo	Mwashuhwa Petros	Dumisani	Samson
Philemon	Mekiseni	Elizabeth	Samuel
Pikaniso Hapson	Mukhanyoni	Cleo	Josiah
Kate	Rivengo	David	Tommy
Mwaronza		Dorothy	Mai Nkomo
		Catherine	Mai Dhliwayo

It looks like Mafofo as the first son inherited both the covenant and associated paraphernalia. When he died, he must have passed it on to Ruben, that is if Ruben was still alive. From Ruben, it went down to Jangwa. Upon Jangwa's death in 2002, this stuff was supposed to go down to Philemon, but Philemon did not want any part of it. It was at this point that the family got together to decide what to do with the paraphernalia. They decided the paraphernalia associated with the covenant needed to be returned to the successors of King Soshangane. Chief Mapungwana and his successors in the Chiping District of present day Zimbabwe were direct descendants of the royal family.

The chief and his spirit medium did not immediately accept the return of the paraphernalia. They asked for time to consult with their own spirit elders and mediums. Eventually, they sent word to the family that they could bring the paraphernalia back. They were also required to bring a bull to be sacrificed at a ceremony evidencing the return of the covenant.

To this day, nobody knows the exact details of the covenant entered into by my ancestor with the king's medium. Likewise, no one knows the implications of returning the associated paraphernalia. Members of the family who had converted to Christianity of course had long distanced themselves from the covenant and the required rituals.

CHRISTIANITY AND THE COVENANT

My grandfather, Hlebayi, converted to Christianity more than one hundred years ago. My father who was born in 1906 followed his father and mother into the Church. To all intents and purposes, therefore, my father was a true Christian, except for the fact that he fathered thirteen children and four of them out of wedlock. This underscores the fact that fornication and adultery in a culture that is at the same time polygamous are difficult to deal with.

His first son, John, was born out of wedlock. We were never told about him until after my father died. Yet of all the children, he was physically the carbon copy of my father. The second one, Temba Dean, was a son from his first marriage. That marriage failed soon after the birth of that first child. My father then got eight children from my mother—seven boys and one girl. My mother was his second wife.

Toward the end of his life, my father fathered three more girls, all from three different young women he befriended. We come from a culture where all children of the father are considered full brothers and sisters, unlike the western cultures where they are considered half brothers and sisters, so we consider ourselves one big happy family.

My father's greatest achievement as a Christian was that he never indulged in the practices then prevalent of consulting witchdoctors and spirit mediums. He also did not believe or practice ancestral worship. In addition to his regular job as the senior agricultural instructor at a government-owned and run agricultural experimental station (Musengezi Experimental Government Farm), he became an ordained minister in the African Methodist Episcopal Church, a church headquartered in Atlanta,

Georgia, in the USA. Indeed, growing up we hosted a number of Black American Bishops visiting the church in the then Southern Rhodesia.

My father passed away in January 1960. Seven months after his passing, my younger brother, Bonani, followed him to the grave. My mother and her family, knowing the history of the family curse, panicked. They started consulting witchdoctors and spirit mediums to protect her children. My mother's fear was that the curse would kill her remaining children one by one. Remember, my father's family had long distanced itself from the covenant. As a result, my family slowly drifted back into the pagan practice of consulting witchdoctors and spirit mediums.

I left home at twenty for Zambia, where I worked for Barclays Bank. Two years later, I left for the UK to study banking and economics. I remained there for some six years and then came to the USA for my Masters in Business Administration (MBA).

Even though I have lived abroad ever since, I was in contact with that lifestyle every time I visited home. I witnessed these practices first hand because the issue of the covenant remained an unsettled one. After independence in 1980, it became possible to consult with spirit mediums and witchdoctors by phone. I came to know one lady who can cure certain types of disorders over the phone. She would ask you to get a cup of water, and she would pray for it and ask the patient to sprinkle the water into the bathtub and bathe. The result was the disorder was gone. She was particularly effective with children who woke up crying every night, like something frightened them in their sleep. I noticed, however, that while the prayers invoked God, there was no mention of Jesus Christ, suggesting that, according to the Bible, these people got their spiritual gifts from the other kingdom.

In our country at the time I was growing up, the tide against Christianity was also rising, fuelled as it were by our struggle for independence, and the suspicion that the Bible had been used by the white man as an instrument of colonialism by the British. It was not unusual for people, especially those involved in the armed struggle to place more faith in our traditional belief system that operates through spirit mediums than in the Bible.

The shared view was that the white man had brought us both oppression and the Bible. These sentiments remained strong even after Zimbabwe's independence in 1980.

The mood has swung the other way since independence however. The young are now very engaged with the church, and the annual Joyous Celebrations testify to this. It is the new face of Christianity in Africa. The problem is there are some parts of our African culture that have proved difficult to discard. These involve rituals associated with the dead. That means that some people in the church continue to participate in these rituals—rituals the Bible considers pagan practices. Even though I do not have firsthand knowledge of this, it is my understanding that the Catholic Church in Zimbabwe and Zambia has endorsed some of these practices and that the church itself might be participating in these practices.

It is this environment that made my uncle, Zikhayi Sithole, such a unique individual in the family. He was the true Christian. Though invited by members of the extended family to attend the ceremony and rituals associated with the surrender of the paraphernalia connected with the covenant, he declined the invitation. That was his practice throughout his life. He believed that the blood of Jesus was all he needed to protect him from any negative effects from the curse. He was for many years the Headmaster of Mount Silinda mission, the hub for learning that served the whole eastern part of Zimbabwe in the early to mid-1900s. He served during the period when the guerilla war in the area was at its worst in the 1970s. Yet through it all, he was able to stand his ground as a Christian. He died in Houston, Texas at the ripe old age of eighty-seven. May he rest in peace.

My issue is here is that the Christian God is a jealous God. One of the verses in the Bible says, *"You shall not bow down to them (other Gods, Idols) or worship them; for I, the LORD your God, am a jealous God, punishing the children for the sin of the parents to the third and fourth generation of those who hate me."*[162] The Christian God does not tolerate the worshipping of idols.

In places like Africa where people are still struggling to break away from their old belief systems that worshipped God through dead ancestors, is it possible that people who continue to partake in these practices are actually inviting a curse into their lives? They are rejecting one belief system but have not totally embraced the Christian God. Are they saved by accepting Jesus Christ as their Lord and Savior while they

---

[162] Exodus 20:5

continue in their old ways? Are they leaving themselves in the clutches of the devil? Is the redemptive power of the blood of Jesus available to them even as they go to church but continue in their pagan practices?

When I reconverted to Christianity, I had the extra baggage of my family history to deal with. I knew becoming a Christian meant rejecting my past, but how do you reject an ancestor to whom you owe your very existence? Had Kuthiya not made peace with the forces of darkness, chances are I and thousands of my clan members would not be here today.

However, Christian teaching is that any covenant other than the Jesus covenant is ungodly. Some of us have accepted that, yet every time I say my standard prayer on the subject that I adopted from Elisha Goodman, I have an undeniable sense of disloyalty to Kuthiya. My standard prayer with respect to cutting ties to my ancestors goes something like this:

> *"No matter what my parents and ancestors did,*
> *Or believed in, contrary to the Living God,*
> *I am not continuing in it so those ancestral powers,*
> *Have no hold over me and my bloodline,*
> *Therefore,*
> *I decree and declare that I am a new creation in Christ Jesus.*
> *Old things have passed away.*
> *Let the blood of redemption speak for me,*
> *Against those ancestral powers,*
> *Laying evil claims against my life and destiny, and*
> *Those invoking them against me."*

I like this prayer because it just about covers it all. It is factual because it addresses my situation. It is fashioned around my known family situation. I like the emphasis on **evil claims** because it does not exactly reject my ancestor. To this day, we are not quite sure what the implications of walking away from a covenant that protected us for more than a century means.

Yet our faith in Jesus and the redemptive power of His shed blood is the one thing we have chosen to hold on to. A nagging feeling remains, however, that we have short changed our ancestor who took action to preserve our bloodline.

Neither can I ignore the fact that the forces of darkness involved here were all that was available to my ancestor and that they were effective in breaking the curse. Because of this sentiment, I deliberately omit prayer lines that would attack my ancestor as such. In my prayers, I focus on ancestral powers laying **evil claims** against my life and destiny. Then again, the question remains: Can the forces of darkness bless you with life?

In Christianity, we sometimes repeat prayers such as "I break and loose myself from every covenant entered into by my ancestors with the forces of darkness by the power in the blood of Jesus" and wonder if this is a helpful prayer line, when that covenant actually gave me life.

Yet the prayer is at the same time disobedient to the Bible that says only the Living God can give me life. The point is when my ancestor did what he did, the Word of God had not spread to my neck of the woods. Christianity did not reach my neck of the woods until the late nineteenth century. Therefore my ancestor did not know that only the Living God has the power to give life, but his conscience and culture guided him. Should he be condemned?

I do not know the answer to this question, but I take comfort in the passage in the Bible that tells us that "all who sin apart from the law will also perish apart from the law, and all who sin under the law will be judged by the law. For it is not those who hear the law who are righteous in God's sight, but it is those who obey the law who will be declared righteous." (Indeed, when Gentiles, who do not have the law, do by nature things required by the law, they are a law for themselves, even though they do not have the law. They show that the requirements of the law are written on their hearts, their consciences also bearing witness, and their thoughts sometimes accusing them, and at other times, even defending them.)

Reading the chapter on spiritual growth in Pastor Rick Warren's book and after my own independent research, I found the chapter a blessing in many ways. It clarified a situation in my mind that I witnessed growing up but did not resolve it. Many Christians in my country never seem to grow spiritually because of this ambivalent stance they maintain with respect to death and their ancestors. An interesting thought though is that, since they were saved when they converted, God probably forgave them their sins, that is, "if the once saved always saved" doctrine in Christianity is correct. However, are these people saved even as they maintain an ambivalent attitude vis-a-vis the Christian God?

Edwin P. Nhliziyo Sr.

Pastor Rick Warren ends that chapter on spiritual growth with another interesting insight. He talks about thinking immature thoughts, which he says are self-centered and self-seeking thoughts. He says babies by nature are completely selfish. They think only about themselves and their needs. They are incapable of giving; they can only receive. I say Amen to that! Amen because, in life, the worst people one can surround oneself with are the self-centered. If you get one of those for a spouse, you better run for dear life! This is just one more nugget to take away from this journey - reading Rick Warren and writing this book.

Even as we celebrate our freedom from the curse, we still wonder what it was that our ancestor gave up to get his life back. What has become apparent over the years is that all our relatives who have tried their hand at business have been met with the same refrain—you will not succeed beyond a certain point. There seemed to be some sort of glass ceiling somewhere, so to speak. Is that what my ancestor gave up? If Kuthiya was the first generation to suffer the curse, my siblings and I are the fourth generation. Then maybe my children have nothing to worry about.